G000294471

A BARTHOLOMEW MAP & GUIDE

WALK EXMOOR
& THE QUANTOCKS

BY LYN RIVERS

JOHN BARTHOLOMEW & SON LTD
EDINBURGH

British Library Cataloguing in Publication Data
Rivers, Lyn
    Walk Exmoor & the Quantocks
    1. England. Exmoor — Visitors' guides
    I. Title
    914.23'8504858
    ISBN 0–7028–0910–1

Published and Printed in Scotland
by John Bartholomew & Son Ltd.,
Duncan Street, Edinburgh EH9 1TA

First edition 1989

Copyright © John Bartholomew & Son Ltd., 1989

Produced for John Bartholomew & Son Ltd
by Curtis Garratt Limited, The Old Vicarage,
Horton cum Studley, Oxford OX9 1BT

Typesetting and maps by Taurus Graphics

Layouts by Taurus Graphics

ISBN 0 7028 0910 1

CONTENTS

KEY MAP FOR THE WALKS

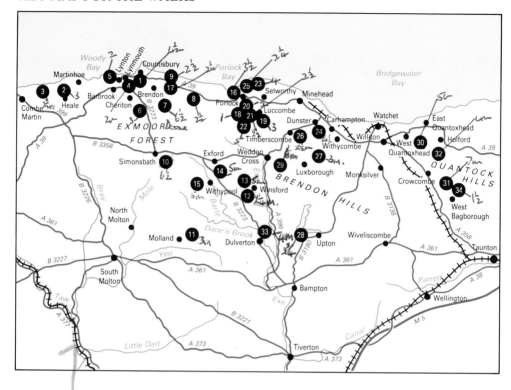

KEY TO SCALE AND MAP SYMBOLS

SCALE 1: 63 360

0 _____ 1 mile

0 _____ 1 km

SCALE 1: 25 000

0 _____ 1 mile

0 _____ 1 km

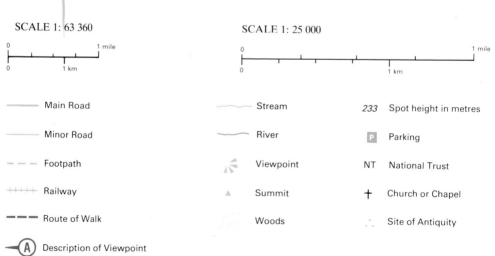

—————— Main Road	—————— Stream	*233* Spot height in metres
—————— Minor Road	—————— River	[P] Parking
– – – Footpath	Viewpoint	NT National Trust
+++++ Railway	▲ Summit	+ Church or Chapel
– – – Route of Walk	Woods	∴ Site of Antiquity
(A) Description of Viewpoint		

1 WALKS AND TOWNS

In compiling a book of walks for an area such as Exmoor, which is not only well known and popular locally, but also a National Park, it would be only too easy simply to repeat the many excellent routes devised by the Park Authority. Usually these are clearly sign-posted, and for many of them, there are descriptive leaflets. On the other hand, even if it was possible, nothing would be achieved by trying to avoid these existing routes entirely. Similarly, one or two of the walks included here follow parts of the Two Moors Way. The Way includes Exmoor and Dartmoor, and provides a connecting link across the county. This contrived long-distance footpath has not become as popular as other designated ways, however, and it is rare to meet walkers whose sole aim has been to complete it. Popular places, such as Dunkery Beacon, which are easily reached from the road over an unmis-takeable path, have been omitted on the grounds that they can easily be found without the help of a book. The routes have been devised to take the walker over some of the lesser-known areas of Exmoor and to show the true character of this beautiful region. Most of them do, however, pass close to a place of refreshment.

The high ground of Exmoor provides the sources for many streams and rivers, from the smallest stream to the waters of the River Exe flowing the length of Devon to the south coast, and these rushing, turbulent water-courses are an added beauty. Steeply wooded combes contrast with the high, bare moorland and, as the valleys become wider and the waters deeper, the villages and towns of Exmoor are found at the old fords and bridges. There is no true town of any size in the region. The market towns of Dulverton, South Molton, and Dunster are still the main centres – pleasant places, and full of history with good local architecture and everything one could want in the way of local shops, inns, and eating places. Dulverton is the headquarters of the National Park Authority, whose centre on the river bank is well worth a visit.

2 EXMOOR NATIONAL PARK

Exmoor is the smallest of the ten original

National Parks, set up in 1949. It occupies an area of some 265 square miles (685 sq km), part in Devon, but largely in Somerset. Exmoor is administered by both county councils with one joint advisory body. It is erroneous to assume that the Park is public property. Apart from land held by the National Trust, Exmoor is in the hands of various individual land-owners, many of them farmers, and the Park Authority is obliged to seek a satisfactory balance between the rights of these owners and the needs of the public.

Exmoor once almost disappeared entirely. Reclaiming vast expanses of moorland was being encouraged to such an extent that, by 1966, it was estimated that only about a quarter of amenity moorland was left. Now that the problem has been highlighted, the situation has become easier, but the Exmoor Society and the Park Authority continue to maintain a necessarily watchful eye.

3 HISTORY OF THE MOOR

The Forest of Exmoor has existed since at least the days of the Norman Conquest. The term 'Forest' in no way refers to woodland. Originally, it described a large area kept solely for the preservation of game, usually deer, over which the king exercised strict and often brutal control. Royal Forests were hunting grounds and, to this day, it is the former 'Forests' which are home to the largest herds of wild deer. Exmoor is the only place in England where red deer still roam.

Over the centuries, the Forest laws relaxed and, in the case of Exmoor, far away from the centre of government, its moorland became 'common land', and the inhabitants acquired grazing and other rights. It was leased out to a Warden who was generally responsible for the management of the Moor and for enforcement of the various rights and laws.

The central Forest area, which lies entirely within Somerset, contains most of the high upland area, the core of Exmoor, and, in many places, the old boundary can still be traced. It is this area that was eventually sold by the Crown in 1818. The purchaser, John Knight, was an industrialist from the Midlands. Over the next eighty years, the Knight family, father and son, were very largely responsible for the creation of Exmoor as we see it today. By using innovative farming methods, sheer hard work, and tenacity, they created farmlands where previously only bare moorland had existed. They built roads and new settlements and, ultimately, they brought some prosperity to what had been a desolate wilderness. The Knights moved to Simonsbath to establish the centre of their domain, and most of today's Simonsbath was built by the family. The large mansion they began was never completed and, finally, it was demolished in 1899. The inn is a popular meeting place, and contains many interesting old prints and photographs of the settlement.

4 EXMOOR AND ITS NEIGHBOURS

The Brendons

This small range of hills is often dismissed by serious walkers as being of little merit. The hills lie within the National Park boundary but they have received very much less attention, from the Park Authority and from the public, than their larger and better-known neighbour. This is partly because there is very little natural moorland left on the Brendons. Large areas are given wholly to forestry, and the overpowering effect of rank upon rank of conifers deters many walkers. It also means that the views are very limited, and one of the main reasons for climbing a hill is for the view. Much of the remainder is farmland, fenced, hedged, and given over to arable crops or grassland. Footpaths exist, but the marvellous feeling of being able to walk for mile after mile without restriction is absent from the Brendons.

Height and some sweeping panoramas are not lacking, however. Lype Hill is second in height only to Dunkery Beacon itself – yet, whereas most people have heard of Dunkery, few could tell you where Lype Hill is located, even though the road passes within a quarter-of-a-mile (400 m) of its unprepossessing summit. It is the highest point of the long ridge of the Brendons which runs from Wheddon Cross in the west to Elworthy in the east. From the western end, where gaps in the hedge, and one layby permit, there are unbroken views over much of Devon and Somerset. The greatest beauty, however, lies in the immediate views of eastern Exmoor, divided by the Exe valley which here begins its long journey south. Winsford Hill and the commanding height of Dunkery make a marvellous backdrop.

The Brendons do not offer the walker long, leg-stretching routes. It would be almost impossible to plot a walk that continued for more than a couple of miles without crossing a road, or without travelling along a metalled surface. It is an area for short, pottering walks – figures-of-eight or a detailed exploration of a valley perhaps. Villages, too, are absent, and there is a corresponding lack of refreshment facilities, although Wheddon Cross and Ralegh's Cross have long had hospitable inns.

There is much pleasure to be had from delving into the many small country lanes and discovering delightful hamlets and unknown corners – Withiel Flory with its little church, Luxborough and Churchtown, the village of Brompton Regis, and the ancient hamlet of Bury.

For the student of industrial archeology, there is a wealth of mining remains, as well as the lost village of Brendon Hill and the dismantled railway that ran from Gupworthy to Watchet. The iron mines of the Brendon Hills realized an output of 52 000 tons in 1877 – the height of their productivity. They were linked to Ebbw Vale in South Wales, where the ore was smelted, but foreign competition led to their decline and ultimate closure, although there was a brief revival in the early 1900s. There was a large mine near Ralegh's Cross, with the miners' village of Brendon Hill situated at over 1200 feet (365 m), the highest village in Somerset. Here, the railway turned to face the sea and ran down an incline, still marked on maps, and still visible through the woodland above Comberow. The railway closed in 1898.

There is wildlife aplenty on the Brendons for those with patience to sit and wait. The early morning and early evening are most profitable when people, too, are usually to be found eating! Hares and deer feed on the farmland, and there are many badger sets for those who know where to look. Above the steep combes, the buzzard and kestrel soar and hover.

The Quantocks

Quantock country is something special. It is too small an area to warrant National Park status in its own right and too far from Exmoor to be included in that Park. Consequently, in this age of organization, the Quantocks are passed by the great majority, despite their close proximity to the M5 and to Taunton.

The Quantocks are, in reality, one hill which runs for about 12 miles (19 km) and is, on average, 3 miles (4¾ km) wide. Although they reach only some 1200 feet (365 m) in height, because of their isolation, the views from the Quantocks are excellent. It is not always possible to pick and choose the days for walking, but the difference between a hazy day and a clear one is extraordinary. On a favourable day you can see right up the valley of the Severn into the heart of England.

Accessibility is a great advantage. There are several wellsited car parks although, in some cases, a little map reading is needed to find them. A good, straight track runs along the crest of the ridge for all its glorious length. Fortunately, cars are prohibited, for it is quite good enough for vehicles, but elderly and less active walkers can enjoy here the views and freedom normally only won after strenuous climbing. Young children in pushchairs or those confined to wheelchairs are also able to use the track. A road crosses the Quantocks from Crowcombe to Nether Stowey, roughly at their centre, and the most popular car parking areas are situated here. The highest ground, at Will's Neck, is a couple of miles to the south-east.

From the smooth, treeless uplands, bracken covered in summer, the Quantocks fall away steeply. The valleys, or combes, are deep, and, to climb out of them can require a considerable though short-lived effort. The contrast in scenery is delightful, for here are the famous wooded combes; Holford and Hodder's Combe on the east, and Crowcombe and Triscombe on the west. The sporadic patches of thorn and rowan quickly give way to stunted oaks but, as the valleys deepen, so the trees acquire stature. Combined with an attractive tinkling stream, they are areas of superb sylvan beauty. Deer are occasionally to be seen in the quieter combes. They were reintroduced in the 1860s, and are now reported to be flourishing.

Inevitably, because the Quantocks provide good riding country, they also make for good hunting country, and stag hunting has been practised here since 1865. This most traditional of English blood sports attracts large crowds to the various meets, and the nature of the Quantocks makes it possible to follow the progress of the hunt from some vantage point or other if you wish. Deer have been exterminated from the Quantocks once before, and many people believe that they would be again if it were not for the tolerance of the farmers and the check put on their numbers by the hunt. Over the centuries, deer have also been poached and, in recent years, this type of illegal killing has again been on the increase. Trapping and killing deer at night can be very cruel and a watchful eye must be kept to deter would-be poachers.

The Quantocks may cover only a small area but they offer among the best walking country and some of the greatest delights to be experienced in England. The one serious threat, that of forestry, has so far been averted. At one time, large areas were proposed for afforestation, but so great was the outcry that several land owners withdrew their consent, and the Forestry Commission is now contained by the area around Quantock Combe and Cockecombe. It would be ideal land for forestry, and it is unfortunate that ideal walking country is also perfect for growing conifers as well as for siting reservoirs. Maintaining open space seems to be a constant battle against first one giant organization and then another.

5 WALKING ON EXMOOR

Exmoor is a friendly place for the inexperienced walker. Provided you stay on public rights of way, it has few dangers and offers great rewards for far less effort than is usually necessary. There are no soaring peaks with sudden rock faces; no precipitous chasms or treacherous slopes. The worst dangers are obvious: scree slopes around Heddon's Mouth and Holdstone; some very steep valley sides; and the cliffs themselves. Nowhere on Exmoor is far from a road or track. Most of Exmoor is not high enough to become covered in clouds for any great length of time; it is more usually misty rain that envelopes the walker, and this is never as dense as cloud and does not come down unexpectedly. Those who set off in dull, wet conditions must expect whatever overtakes them. On such days it is the river valleys and combes that offer the best and safest rewards.

On the other hand, the area known as The Chains contains some of the highest and loneliest ground within the National Park. No road crosses its sodden heights and there are few paths. It is notorious for its bogs, and the complete absence of distinguishing landmarks makes it easy to lose all sense of direction. The Chains lie inland from Lynton and, even for farming, the area has been largely abandoned. None of the walks in this book crosses The Chains. One safe excursion to satisfy the curious is to park in the layby on the Challacombe to Simonsbath road and walk up the track to Pinkery Pond. This should be quite enough for most people.

Some advice for walkers

Before setting off on any expedition there are certain guidelines which you should follow and which will help the enjoyment and success of the day.

For safety's sake:
(a) Tell someone where you are going, or leave a note in your car as to the direction you have taken.
(b) Study the map properly before setting off so that you have a good idea where you are going should you lose the map.
(c) Take money and food in case of an emergency.
(d) Ensure that everyone is properly dressed. Bare feet or sandals are no protection against adders, stones, or barbed wire. Even in warm weather, it is advisable to take a windproof because the temperature can drop markedly as you gain height, and the wind can be unexpectedly cold.

Never be too ambitious. Remember, there is always the return journey and your walk should be geared to the weakest member of the party. Carrying youngsters for the last few miles, for example, is not likely to improve anyone's temper. A walk should be a pleasure not an endurance test, and it is far better to turn back than to continue and walk further than you can cope with comfortably. Try to involve all members of the party in the planning and in map reading. Not only should this increase their enjoyment and knowledge but it should also encourage participation and responsibility. It is inadvisable for only one member of a group to know exactly where they are and where they plan to go.

To get the most out of Exmoor, the Brendons, and the Quantocks, walks should be planned as leisurely affairs with plenty of time to stop and enjoy the views and watch wildlife. These areas have so much to offer, it would be a pity to rush your walk. By trying to do too much, some of the best things that Exmoor has to offer will be missed. There is always another day.

COUNTISBURY TO ROCKFORD

$4\frac{1}{2}$ miles ($7\frac{1}{4}$ km) Moderate; 1 steep section, not suitable after heavy rain

Nowhere on Exmoor is there a more dramatic or more beautiful valley than that of the East Lyn. 'Valley' is not quite the right word; here, the river has worn for itself a gorge, a cleft – a 'cleave' in Exmoor language. Short, scrubby oaks clothe the sides, turning to a myriad of bronzes and golds in the autumn. Brown trout play in the waters, and dippers, wagtails, the occasional heron, and many other birds haunt the river and its banks.

From the heights, the nature of the cleave can be appreciated, with views down towards Lynmouth, or across the top to the central uplands of the Moor. From the valley floor, the walk is sylvan, and there is an opportunity to study the intimate details of nature, where you can take as long as you like to potter happily along the riverbank. After you have crossed the A39 at Countisbury, there is a great contrast in scenery as the path comes out on the headland high above Lyn-

mouth Bay. Spectacular views along the coast and across the Bristol Channel to Wales are rewarding, and the fresh sea air can be welcome after the exertion of climbing up out of the cleave. It may seem that the walk is being extended, but the distance involved is minimal, the views magnificent, and the path much safer and preferable to ending the walk along the main road.

A The Barna Barrow car park takes its name from the archeological site lying in the fields to the east. At 1057 feet (322 m), the car park is well sited on what are the highest headlands in North Devon.

B Situated on an ancient crossing point of the East Lyn river, Rockford has a popular inn, a craft shop, and café. Apart from the inn car park, there is no space for cars.

C A bench provides a welcome rest from which to appreciate the lovely views over the steeply wooded valleys of the East Lyn and Hoaroak Waters. A level path leads out to Horner's Neck directly opposite Watersmeet and is worth visiting.

D Countisbury is a small cluster of quaint old cottages – note the round chimneys – a church, and an ancient inn known for centuries as the Blue Ball Inn. It was

the stopping point for coaches negotiating the notorious steep hill out of Lynmouth.

E Butter Hill at 991 feet (303 m) is an airy height on the headland known as the Foreland – the most northerly point of North Devon. The little building close by was a wireless station, and there are views across the Channel and inland across to Brendon Common, Hollerday Hill, and Lynmouth.

Over

0   1 mile

0   1 km

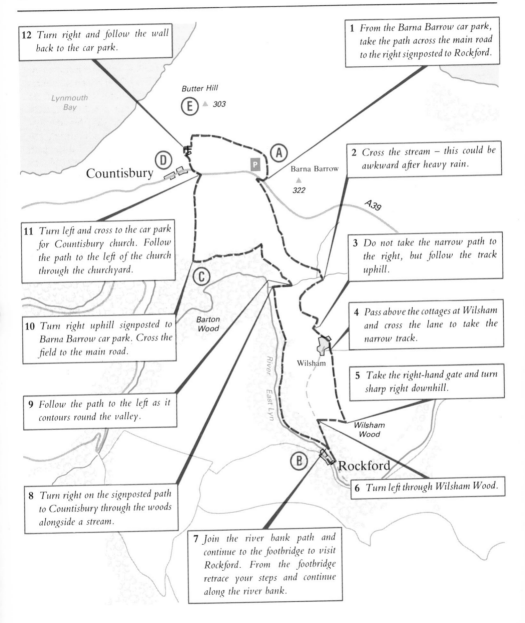

12 *Turn right and follow the wall back to the car park.*

1 *From the Barna Barrow car park, take the path across the main road to the right signposted to Rockford.*

Butter Hill

Ⓔ ▲ *303*

Lynmouth Bay

Ⓐ

Countisbury Ⓓ

Ⓟ

Barna Barrow

▲ *322*

A39

2 *Cross the stream – this could be awkward after heavy rain.*

11 *Turn left and cross to the car park for Countisbury church. Follow the path to the left of the church through the churchyard.*

Ⓒ

3 *Do not take the narrow path to the right, but follow the track uphill.*

4 *Pass above the cottages at Wilsham and cross the lane to take the narrow track.*

10 *Turn right uphill signposted to Barna Barrow car park. Cross the field to the main road.*

Barton Wood

Wilsham

5 *Take the right-hand gate and turn sharp right downhill.*

River East Lyn

9 *Follow the path to the left as it contours round the valley.*

Wilsham Wood

Ⓑ *Rockford*

8 *Turn right on the signposted path to Countisbury through the woods alongside a stream.*

6 *Turn left through Wilsham Wood.*

7 *Join the river bank path and continue to the footbridge to visit Rockford. From the footbridge retrace your steps and continue along the river bank.*

Walk 2
HEDDON ESTATE AND HEALE
3 miles (5 km) Moderate

This walk takes you away from the crowds that throng the Hunters Inn valley and who stroll down the broad track to Heddon's Mouth, with its stony beach and restored limekiln. Instead, it enters a quiet area, seldom seen and full of peaceful beauty. The Ladies Mile is a delightful grassy track, and the scenery changes from woodland to moorland, riverside, and farmland.

Park on the Trentishoe road either in a former quarry or on the grass verges at Rhydda Bank.

1 Begin at the moss-covered wooden post on the road verge. Follow this level grassy path through woodland.

11 Just beyond a slate gatepost and a huge lime tree on the river bank, turn right uphill to the road at Rhydda Bank.

10 Turn left back up the valley.

2 Turn left downhill to reach the road, and turn left for a short distance.

9 The path crosses a track and passes through the yard of 'Vention Cottage' to a wooden footbridge across the stream.

South Dean

Rhydda Bank Cross

Parsonage Wood

National Trust

Invention Wood

Ladies Mile

River Heddon

A

8 A bridle track joins from the right. Continue downwards and bear round to the left.

B

Heale

7 Turn left directly opposite the cleft that is Heddon's Mouth. Follow the track between the hedge and a new wire fence.

3 Take the track to the right signposted to Heale and Hunters Inn.

4 Turn right again to the footbridge with a stile and gate on the far side and follow the path upwards to the left.

5 The path curves through two gates to join an unmade lane. Turn left and follow the lane into a field above the woods.

6 Follow the beech hedge on the right until its junction with a ruined wall and hedge.

A Exmoor has a great variety of trees and the woodland here is particularly fine. At the junction, there is a stunted copper beech, rowan, elder, birch, oak, thorn, and sycamore. There are also some wild raspberries.

B As the path levels out, look to the right. The opposite side of the valley is roughly ridged, the result either of the weather or of former cultivation and, in spring, it is carpeted with primroses.

12

HOLDSTONE DOWN

2¼ miles (3½ km) Moderate

0 _____ 1 mile
0 _____ 1 km

Some very dramatic coastal scenery is found within the Exmoor National Park boundary, and here the land falls in bold sweeps known as a hog's back formation. There are no secrets on the Holdstone Down walk; the summit is obvious and the route never in doubt, and for most of the way, it is clearly visible. But the views are among the best, and the rewards are quite out of proportion to the minimal effort involved. Elderly or less energetic members of a group party may be left in a car park that enjoys unrivalled views inland across Exmoor to The Chains.

6 Follow the broad track gently uphill as it turns away around the lower slopes of Holdstone Down.

7 At the main road by the bungalows turn right and follow the road back to the car park.

Girt Down

B

Holdstone Down

C

The Glass Box

NT

Moorlands

Holdstone Hill

349

Stones

A

National Trust

P

Trentishoe Down

5 A signpost indicates that this is the coast path. Turn right.

1 Leave the quarry car park by the signposted route, and follow a clear path uphill to a smaller disused quarry.

4 The path becomes faint but meets a ruined stone wall. Turn left, then cross the wall through a gap and follow the path downhill.

3 From the summit, follow a stony path to the left, downhill.

2 A narrower path strikes uphill for a short distance to the summit of Holdstone Down

A The summit of Holdstone Down is a magnificent viewpoint, marked with an untidy heap of stones. Similar heaps adorn the Great Hangman to the left, and Trentishoe Down to the right, neither of which is as high as Holdstone.

B There are impressive views of Girt Down rising to the Hangman, and down into the steep cleft of Sherrycombe.

C The bungalow here offers refreshments. Note the aptly named 'Glass Box' bungalow opposite.

13

WATERSMEET

2 miles (3¼ km) Easy

Some walks seem so obvious that it is surprising they are not better known. The track alongside the Hoaroak Water is popular, but the higher section of this route is used only as a part of a longer walk to Lynmouth. Together, the two paths make a delightful round journey, with excellent home-made offerings available at Watersmeet National Trust shop as an added pleasure.

The views above Myrtleberry Cleave are among the best of the East Lyn valley, and it is here that one would linger on a sunny day before plunging down through the woodland. The East Lyn and Hoaroak rivers meet at Watersmeet (hence the name), and here, too, it seems unnecessary to hurry. Only the water does that, rushing over the boulders and cascading into pools, the haunt of dippers and wagtails. The sound of the water drowns any noise from the road above and, perhaps fortunately, it is not possible to reach Watersmeet except by climbing down from the road. A car park on its banks would dramatically alter the spot.

The trees are mainly sessile oak with some whitebeam – the less usual Devon variety – and, on the estate, the rare Irish spurge can be found. The whole Watersmeet estate is laid out with well-signposted paths and tracks, many of which were originally made by charcoal burners. A short distance up the East Lyn river is a large lime kiln which has been restored recently. It is unusual to find such a substantial kiln so far inland and apparently on the way to nowhere.

Strolling back along the river bank is a gentle, easy climb.

Note that at Point 5, where the path comes out suddenly on to the main road, make sure that children and dogs are under control.

A Two Iron Age camp sites have been discovered on this prominent hillside. Myrtleberry South Camp is the higher, to the left of the path. Myrtleberry North lies just above the woodland and is better sited.

B The view is down the valley of the East Lyn to Lynton and Lynmouth, and the blue of Lynmouth Bay beyond. The deep cleft in the cliffs makes the view all the more dramatic. The foreground is dominated by the steeply wooded slopes of Myrtleberry Cleave on the left bank and Wester Wood surmounted by Windhill opposite. Even on a dull, misty day, the view is worthwhile.

C Watersmeet House was built originally as the fishing lodge to the Glenthorne Estate. It is now a National Trust shop and restaurant.

D There is a fine view point of the waterfalls from the end of the short length of path. It can be slippery!

Over

0   1 mile

0   1 km

4 *Turn right down to Watersmeet.*

5 *The path emerges suddenly on the main road. Cross to the parking layby opposite. The path leaves from the left-hand corner.*

6 *Cross the two bridges to reach Watersmeet House.*

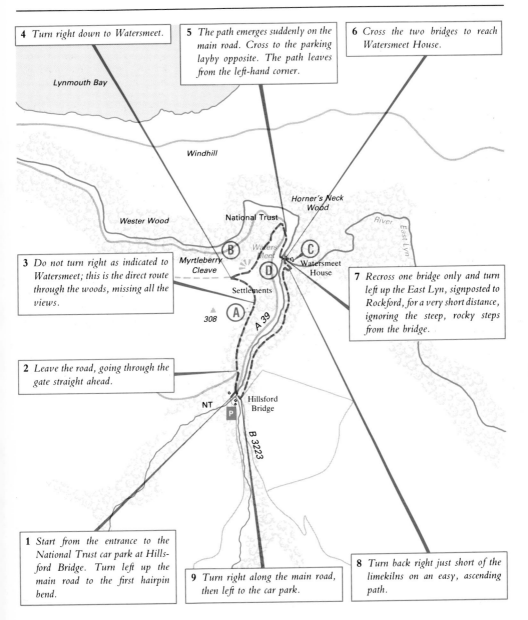

Lynmouth Bay

Windhill

Horner's Neck Wood

Wester Wood

National Trust

3 *Do not turn right as indicated to Watersmeet; this is the direct route through the woods, missing all the views.*

Myrtleberry Cleave

Settlements

Watersmeet House

7 *Recross one bridge only and turn left up the East Lyn, signposted to Rockford, for a very short distance, ignoring the steep, rocky steps from the bridge.*

308

A 39

River East Lyn

2 *Leave the road, going through the gate straight ahead.*

NT

Hillsford Bridge

P

B 3223

1 *Start from the entrance to the National Trust car park at Hillsford Bridge. Turn left up the main road to the first hairpin bend.*

9 *Turn right along the main road, then left to the car park.*

8 *Turn back right just short of the limekilns on an easy, ascending path.*

15

Walk 5

HOLLERDAY HILL

2 miles (3km) Easy

Few walks give such great rewards for so little effort as this one. There is a bewildering choice of paths around the wooded slopes overlooking Lynton on one side and the sea on the other. Hollerday House was the home of George Newnes, a prominent Victorian publisher who was responsible for the Town Hall, the narrow-gauge Lynton Railway, and the Cliff Railway. The house was destroyed shortly after his death and the grounds are now the property of the Town Council.

9 *Turn right, climbing uphill gently.*

10 *All routes lead to Lynton here; turn right on a tarmac path.*

11 *Cross the cliff railway and continue to Lynton, or turn down left to Lynmouth on the signposted lane.*

8 *Ignore the 'coast path' signpost and go downhill to a small stone-built shelter.*

7 *Turn downhill inland alongside the wall and right on the main path.*

1 *Park in Lynton and walk up the road alongside the Town Hall, bearing left, signposted to Hollerday Hill.*

6 *At the signpost, turn left uphill and on to the summit.*

2 *Turn left, back across the town, past Honeypot Cottage.*

5 *Exit left; go up more log steps, and turn right on the path.*

4 *Zig-zag: second left just before a clearing, then right, then left up a flight of log steps to the former tennis court area.*

3 *Turn right, signposted to a picnic area.*

A The summit of Hollerday Hill is a marvellous, airy place with comfortable grassy areas. Inland are the heights of Exmoor; seawards are Foreland Point to the east, and Woody Bay and Martinhoe to the west. Below is Lynton with the steeply wooded cleaves to the East and West Lyn rivers.

B Not far from the stone shelter overlooking the cricket pitch and the Valley of Rocks with its wild goats, is an elderly sign warning that it is a felony wilfully to start a fire, but the penalties incurred have been lost.

C The Cliff Railway has provided a link between Lynton and Lynmouth since 1890, and it runs as smoothly today as it did when it was first opened. The two cars are controlled by a water tank; the length is 901 feet (275 m 62 cm) and gradient 1 in 1¾.

FARLEY WATER

0   1 mile

0   1 km

3 miles (5 km) Moderate; wet in places

The unfenced road from Simonsbath to Lynton crosses the heights of Brendon Common, giving the motorist some of the best possible views from the many car parks provided. For the walker, it gives access to remoter and bleaker areas of Exmoor. Farley Water lies, hidden and secret, out of sight from the road. Because the moor here is open and uncultivated, there are few paths. Those that do exist often prove to be sheep tracks, petering out and leaving the walker stranded in a sea of heather.

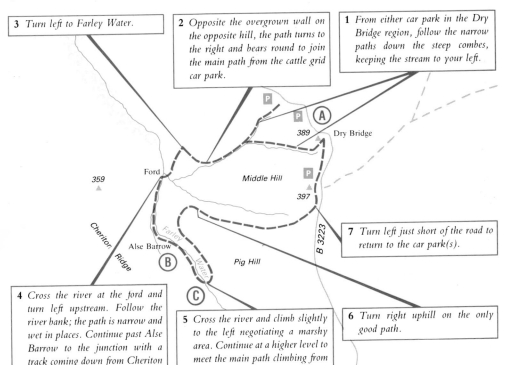

3 *Turn left to Farley Water.*

2 *Opposite the overgrown wall on the opposite hill, the path turns to the right and bears round to join the main path from the cattle grid car park.*

1 *From either car park in the Dry Bridge region, follow the narrow paths down the steep combes, keeping the stream to your left.*

389   Dry Bridge

Ford

359

Middle Hill

397

Cheriton Ridge

Alse Barrow

Farley Water

Pig Hill

B 3223

7 *Turn left just short of the road to return to the car park(s).*

4 *Cross the river at the ford and turn left upstream. Follow the river bank; the path is narrow and wet in places. Continue past Alse Barrow to the junction with a track coming down from Cheriton Ridge.*

5 *Cross the river and climb slightly to the left negotiating a marshy area. Continue at a higher level to meet the main path climbing from the ford.*

6 *Turn right uphill on the only good path.*

A From the road, there are views across the fringes of the moor to Lynton and Lynmouth Bay with the heights of the Great Hangman to the left.

B The valley of Farley Water is deep and wooded in its lower section. By the ford, there is a beautiful oak tree. After heavy rain, it may be difficult to cross this lovely moorland water, in which case, follow the path down the bank.

Alse Barrow is a natural height with a dry valley on one side and Farley Water on the other. There is no clear path over its bracken-clad summit, and the views are not materially better.

C Farley Water is particularly delightful in this stretch – full of pools and waterfalls – even a 'Mermaid's Pool' on hot days!

17

DOONE VALLEY

6½ miles (10½ km) Moderate

0 _____ 1 mile
0 _____ 1 km

This is a more interesting route than the standard Doone Valley walk that follows the broad trail from Malmsmead. The approach over the top gives a combination of open moorland, wooded combe, river bank, and historical romance. It should be saved for a clear day in spring or autumn when the views across the barren uplands are far-reaching.

The romance of Lorna Doone is a curious phenomenon. Why should a long and, in places, prosy novel have inspired such a tourist boom? Its author was surprised at its success, which continues unabated, although few of the tourists who come by the coach load have ever read *Lorna Doone*.

3 *Turn right at the junction of tracks.*

4 *At the stone wall and gate, turn left downhill; do not go through the gate. The path is indistinct for a short distance.*

5 *Follow the path to the right, downhill into the woodland, to meet the main path up the Doone Valley.*

2 *Continue along the well-defined track ignoring the left fork, and the right-hand signpost to the Doone Valley.*

Malmsmead Hill

Cloud Farm

Ⓑ

389

Ⓒ

Dry Bridge

397 Ⓟ

Middle Hill

Doone Valley

Badgworthy Wood

Badgworthy

Ⓐ

1 *From the disused quarry car park the track is signposted to Brendon Common. An alternative track leads up from Dry Bridge. At their junction, the Doone Valley is signposted.*

Brendon Common

Hoccombe Combe

Ⓓ

6 *Turn left downstream to the memorial. Then retrace your steps and continue up the valley on the broad tourist path.*

Water

Hoccombe Water

9 *Turn left back to the car park.*

8 *Go through the gate in the stone wall, and keep straight ahead on the track over the moorland to rejoin the main path.*

7 *Leave the Doone Valley and follow the higher path into Hoccombe Combe. Continue uphill, ignoring the path to Hoccombe Water.*

A Brendon Common, at 1353 feet (412 m), is one of the higher areas, and ahead, marked by a post, is Malmsmead Hill.

B Before turning downhill, look down the lower Doone Valley at Cloud Farm, a rare view.

C A memorial stone to R D Blackmore was erected here in 1969, 100 years after the publication of *Lorna Doone*.

D Hoccombe Combe is the site of a medieval village. It is here, if anywhere, that the Doones were supposed to have had their stronghold. The low grassy ruins are to the left of the path behind the ridge.

OARE AND YENWORTHY

2½ miles (4 km) Moderate

Within the space of this relatively short walk are the heights of Yenworthy Common at 1237 feet (377 m), Clannel Combe, the river-bank of Oare Water, the famous Exmoor church at Oare (with its associations with *Lorna Doone*, R.D. Blackmore's famous Exmoor novel), and a wide range of superb views in every direction.

Look for the car park to the left of the A39 beyond County Gate, just short of the drive to Yen-worthy Lodge, from which there are panoramic views including Holdstone, Hollerday and Malms-mead Hills, the heights of Exmoor across the valley, Dunkery and Bossington Hill, with the coast of Wales across the Bristol Channel.

1 *Follow the track downhill keeping right at the fork.*

2 *At the fingerpost, turn right up hill. Through the gate the track fades, but walk diagonally uphill aiming to the right of the trees on the summit.*

3 *Cross the busy main road with care. Follow the track beyond the beech trees, signposted to Oare church, and keep to the track around the head of Deddy Combe.*

5 *Turn right on the road, then right immediately past the entrance to Oare House, signposted to Yen-worthy. Watch for the yellow mark where the track bears to the left, and continue straight up the hill back to the car park.*

4 *Turn right downhill, following the yellow marks.*

A To the left is Glenthorne, al-though the house cannot be seen. The coastal footpath contours below to Culbone on the right.

B Beyond the signpost, North Common opens out, with the valley of the Weir Water and Alderman's Barrow opposite.

C The hamlet of Oare lies below, with its church and manor. It was in the church that Lorna Doone was shot during her wedding, but the church has been extended and altered since Blackmore wrote his novel. The wooded sweep of the Oare Water Valley to the left is particularly fine.

D Oare church and manor again make an attractive group with the open moorland behind becoming ever more impressive as height is gained.

GLENTHORNE

2½ miles (4 km) Moderate

The Glenthorne estate is uniquely beautiful on the North Devon/Somerset coast. The boundary runs down the centre – Coscombe. The estate was the creation of the Reverend Walter Halliday. He was left a substantial legacy in the 1870s with which to purchase land and, moving from the Isle of Wight, he chose Glenthorne. The Victorians were great builders, and the Rev. Halliday was not at all deterred by the steepness of the combe. He created a series of drives and walks, with cottages, estate buildings, and a lodge with imposing gateposts surmounted by boars' heads. Until 1983, the estate was still in the ownership of the Halliday family, and the public had only restricted access. In that year the estate was sold and the National Trust was able to purchase the cliffs but not the entire estate. A series of walks has now been devised by the National Park Authority, which publishes a leaflet about the estate.

The walk given here includes the best of the views but omits the steep climbs back up to the main road by making use of the original carriage drive.

Sisters' Fountain, which is a natural spring surmounted by a stone cross, was so called after the Reverend Halliday's nieces. Below it is a sign warning that adders are breeding – a deterrent to trespassers perhaps?

County Gate provides ample parking in the National Park car park. The former toll house, that marks the county boundary, was said to give the keeper the distinction of being the only man to sleep in two counties – his head in Devon and his feet in Somerset!

A This is one of the few places from which Glenthorne House is visible. The house was carefully sited, almost on the beach, and occupies a spectacular position. It has been described as Victorian Gothic.

B Combe Corner is a magnificent view point, missed by those who take the short cut. The valley lies below, although Glenthorne House is out of sight.

C The view from Cosgate Hill is almost entirely inland. The land drops steeply to the valley of the East Lyn and, almost directly opposite, are Malmsmead and the 'Doone Valley'. Behind, the moor climbs steadily to Brendon Common, and, to the left, Dunkery Beacon.

Over

0   1 mile
0   1 km

6 Turn right, ignoring the grassy path ahead signposted to the main road. Follow the drive uphill.

5 Turn left in front of the main gates and lodge house, over the cattle grid.

4 Take the small path to the right signposted to Wingate Combe and Sister's Fountain. There is a short descent to the fountain, then the path climbs gently to meet the road down to Glenthorne.

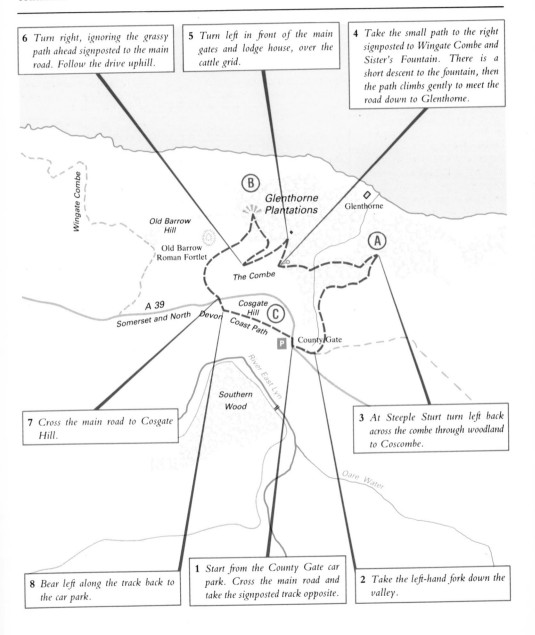

Wingate Combe

Old Barrow Hill

Old Barrow Roman Fortlet

The Combe

(B)

Glenthorne Plantations

Glenthorne

(A)

A 39
Somerset and North Devon Coast Path

Cosgate Hill

(C)

County Gate

River East Lyn

Southern Wood

Oare Water

7 Cross the main road to Cosgate Hill.

3 At Steeple Sturt turn left back across the combe through woodland to Coscombe.

8 Bear left along the track back to the car park.

1 Start from the County Gate car park. Cross the main road and take the signposted track opposite.

2 Take the left-hand fork down the valley.

SIMONSBATH AND BARLE VALLEY

6½ miles (10½ km) Easy; one awkward stretch

Simonsbath is strategically important as the crossing of main routes over Exmoor, and was also the centre of the ancient Forest. But, until the coming of the Knights, there was nothing here except Simonsbath House, now a hotel. The Knights built almost everything else and are buried in the churchyard.

The walk follows one of Exmoor's lovely streams with a good variety of views. It is a good winter walk because the valley is sheltered.

---

2 *Cross to the small gate by a group of outbuildings in disrepair opposite the Exmoor Forest Hotel, and follow the path as it climbs through the wood and then slightly down to the right to join a main path from the road by a large signboard.*

3 *Turn left uphill following the red marks and the seemingly circuitous path.*

4 *Look for a red mark on a gate on the right opposite a forestry track. Go through it and into a field. Follow the hedge on the left and through double gates at the far end. Bear right across the field to another gate. Follow the hedge and red marks to Winstitchen Farm on the left.*

5 *Turn right away from Winstitchen Farm and follow the field hedge through two more gates.*

6 *Where the hedge ends in a small copse of fir trees, the path crosses to the White Water side and descends beside a little tree-lined valley.*

7 *Continue across the White Water and up the farm track.*

Simonsbath

B 3358

B 3226

B 3223

Winstitchen Farm

A

E

Wheal Eliza

339

Flexbarrow

River Barle

B

Picked Stones

Cow Castle

D

Pickedstones Farm

White Water

C

Two Moors Way

1 *From the entry road to the car park, walk downhill (right) on the B3223 for a short distance.*

A Birch Cleave Wood is a beech wood planted by the Knight family in the 1800s on ground that rises to almost 1200 feet (365 m).

B The former quarry workings beside the White Water provide a level grassy area surrounded by trees, with a ruin to add to the charm.

C Moorland opens out with a view to the beauty spot of Landacre Bridge.

Over

8 *At Pickedstones Farm, cross the farmyard and follow the farm road. Bear right through the gate following red marks. Cross the field and go through another gate on to open moorland.*

9 *Continue on the track for a short distance, and then turn right downhill at the red post. (The track continues to Landacre Bridge.)*

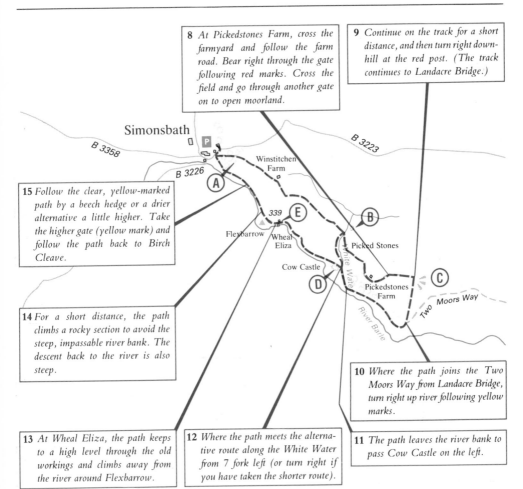

15 *Follow the clear, yellow-marked path by a beech hedge or a drier alternative a little higher. Take the higher gate (yellow mark) and follow the path back to Birch Cleave.*

14 *For a short distance, the path climbs a rocky section to avoid the steep, impassable river bank. The descent back to the river is also steep.*

10 *Where the path joins the Two Moors Way from Landacre Bridge, turn right up river following yellow marks.*

13 *At Wheal Eliza, the path keeps to a high level through the old workings and climbs away from the river around Flexbarrow.*

12 *Where the path meets the alternative route along the White Water from 7 fork left (or turn right if you have taken the shorter route).*

11 *The path leaves the river bank to pass Cow Castle on the left.*

D Cow Castle is a superb example of an Iron Age fort dominating the upper Barle. In places the earthworks on the summit are up to 10 feet (3 m) high and stretch for 1000 feet (300 m). This is an outstanding viewpoint.

E Wheal Eliza mine is now derelict and few traces of the buildings remain. A 250-foot (75-m) shaft was sunk in search of copper but was not very successful. A widower who lived in the cottage which once stood by the White Water was supposed to have murdered his daughter because he wanted to remarry. When the place on the moor where he had buried her was in danger of discovery, it is said that he flung her body down the mine and fled to Wales. Justice caught up with him, however, and he was hanged at Taunton in 1858.

MOLLAND AND ANSTEY'S COMMON

3 miles (5 km) Moderate; wet in places

From the southern ridge of Exmoor, the land falls down to the rich farmland of Devon. To the north is the bleak, barren moor rising to the sombre heights of Dunkery; to the south, on a clear day, the equally sombre heights of Dartmoor loom. Between is a landscape that is essentially English and has remained virtually unchanged for centuries. The pattern of small fields, hedgerows, copses, hamlets, and church towers is what the rest of the country used to look like before mechanization and intensive farming altered the face of England.

The views from the ridge, which runs from North Molton down into Dulverton, are superb even for the car-bound, and quite different from anything else Exmoor has to offer. The sea plays no part, and not much of the rest of the moor is visible, but the contrast between untamed upland and pastoral lowland is there all the same.

The Ordnance Survey map clearly shows a path from Molland village to Smallacombe linking with the Bremley Cross route. It is not clear under foot, however, and adds little to the walk except unrewarding exertion.

Bremley Cross is reached via a few miles of country lanes. From the church, continue straight on, past the chapel, signposted Stone Cross. Here turn left to Bremley Cross. The parking is unofficial on the broad grass junction, and

an alternative would be to park on Molland Common close to Anstey's Gate.

Molland is a delightful village, relatively unspoilt and unknown. It has many charming cottages, an ancient church, and an inn that has changed little over the centuries and which is called, most inappropriately the London Inn. The inn is still owned by the local lord of the manor. The church has a rare Georgian interior, with boxed pews and three-decker pulpit, that has managed to survive virtually intact. The supporting pillars lean at a definite angle, but this no longer gives cause for concern. The church is well known for its team of bellringers whose certificates line the bell-chamber.

A Anstey's Gate on the ridge road is a popular parking spot with views out across rural Devon. From here, a clear track runs down alongside the bank to meet the farm road to Brimblecombe.

B Dartmoor can be seen in the distance across the lowlands of Devon.

C Anstey's Gully is a lovely wooded combe with a moorland stream beginning its journey from Exmoor.

Over

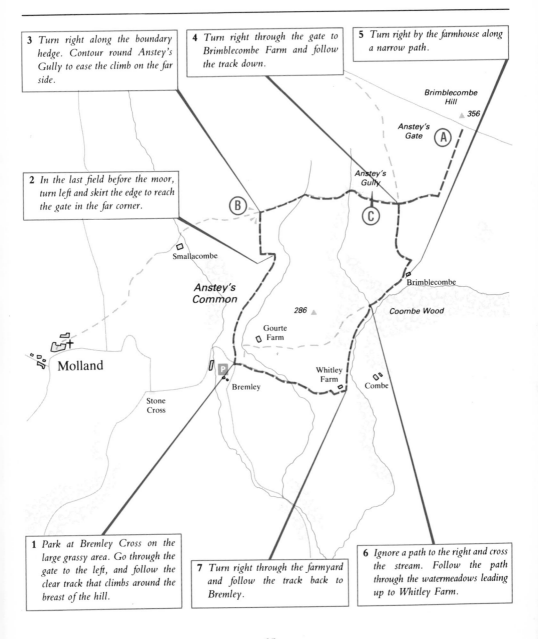

3 *Turn right along the boundary hedge. Contour round Anstey's Gully to ease the climb on the far side.*

4 *Turn right through the gate to Brimblecombe Farm and follow the track down.*

5 *Turn right by the farmhouse along a narrow path.*

2 *In the last field before the moor, turn left and skirt the edge to reach the gate in the far corner.*

1 *Park at Bremley Cross on the large grassy area. Go through the gate to the left, and follow the clear track that climbs around the breast of the hill.*

7 *Turn right through the farmyard and follow the track back to Bremley.*

6 *Ignore a path to the right and cross the stream. Follow the path through the watermeadows leading up to Whitley Farm.*

Brimblecombe Hill

356

Anstey's Gate (A)

Anstey's Gully

(B)

(C)

Smallacombe

Brimblecombe

Anstey's Common

286

Coombe Wood

Gourte Farm

Whitley Farm

Combe

Molland

Bremley

P

Stone Cross

25

CARATACUS STONE AND WINSFORD

2¼ miles (3½ km) Easy; muddy in places

Here is a short walk that combines many of the elements of the more ambitious routes, and has much to commend it. Starting on open moorland, where parking is possible, it takes in one of the oldest monuments on Exmoor.

From moorland, it passes to light woodland where quiet walkers may be rewarded with a sighting of the red deer. The route then skirts the forest at the top of the valley. The views over Winsford towards the Brendon Hills make a pleasant backdrop to the equally pleasant immediate surroundings. This makes a more peaceful alternative to the popular walk up Winsford Hill itself, where the summit is only yards away from the road.

A The origins and purpose of the Caratacus Stone remain a mystery after much detailed research over many years. Until relatively recent times, even the inscription was debated, but it has finally been deciphered as *Carataci Nepus* meaning 'Kinsman of Caratacus'. Historians believe that it was originally a boundary stone marking the domain of a minor chieftain shortly after the departure of the Romans. The stone weighs almost 800 pounds (363 kg) and leans at 8 degrees. When it was dislodged in 1936, the stone was re-erected at exactly the same angle as before. Without its inappropriate shelter, it would be quite easy to miss the stone altogether.

Over

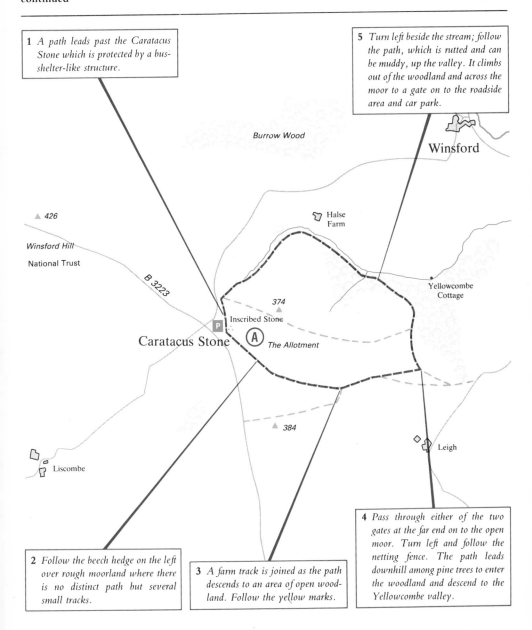

1 *A path leads past the Caratacus Stone which is protected by a bus-shelter-like structure.*

5 *Turn left beside the stream; follow the path, which is rutted and can be muddy, up the valley. It climbs out of the woodland and across the moor to a gate on to the roadside area and car park.*

Burrow Wood

Winsford

▲ 426

Winsford Hill

National Trust

B 3223

Halse Farm

Yellowcombe Cottage

374 ▲

P Inscribed Stone

Caratacus Stone (A) The Allotment

▲ 384

Liscombe

Leigh

2 *Follow the beech hedge on the left over rough moorland where there is no distinct path but several small tracks.*

3 *A farm track is joined as the path descends to an area of open woodland. Follow the yellow marks.*

4 *Pass through either of the two gates at the far end on to the open moor. Turn left and follow the netting fence. The path leads downhill among pine trees to enter the woodland and descend to the Yellowcombe valley.*

WINSFORD TO NETHERCOTE UP THE RIVER EXE
5 miles (8 km) Moderate

Winsford is one of Exmoor's tourist meccas. Here, the Exe valley broadens out and the wilderness of Exmoor retreats. The village is famous for the seven bridges crossing the stream that here joins with the Exe.

The Royal Oak is a well-known inn that has dispensed hospitality for centuries. At one time flitches of bacon and ham were hung in the cavernous fireplace above the fire, a sight once commonplace on Exmoor. The picturesque thatched building is much photographed and a popular meeting place in both senses of the word. A large car park is sited in the centre of the village where there are several establishments offering refreshment, and a well-stocked village store cum post office. The church is perched above the village, close to the start of the footpath.

Woodland walks are best undertaken in autumn or spring. The walk from Winsford is particularly lovely as the trees turn colour. The views from the heights of Bye Hill up the Exe valley are very rewarding.

The direction in which you walk does not always matter, the views being equally attractive either way. To get the best from this route, however, it is essential to follow the high-level path up the valley and to return along the river bank. Thus, you walk towards the heights of Exmoor, looking up the valley of the River Exe. The descent leads down to the woodlands bordering the river. The return walk becomes more shut-in as the valley deepens and, although the nearby scenery is pleasant, there are no views. The farm track provides good, dry walking but the last section is over a footpath which meanders among the alders and willows of the valley floor.

There are no problems on this walk with only the gentlest of inclines unless the Hope Cottage short-cut is used. This is a little arduous, because it is intended for wheeled traffic rather than for walkers.

A Bye Hill at 1201 feet (366 m) provides a vantage point from which to look across the Exe valley to Dunkery. To the right are the Brendon Hills, and below is the valley as it winds its way down from Exford, with Room Hill and Curr Cleave prominent.

B Many of the Exmoor walks have alternative starts; there are several quiet car parks known only to a few. Winsford is the obvious start and finish but, for those who prefer to avoid the centres of civilization, there is a small parking area off the Exford road, reached by turning left over the farm bridge just beyond Hope Cottage. From here, a new track climbs uphill to Bye Hill where it joins the path from Winsford.

Over

0   1 mile
0   1 km

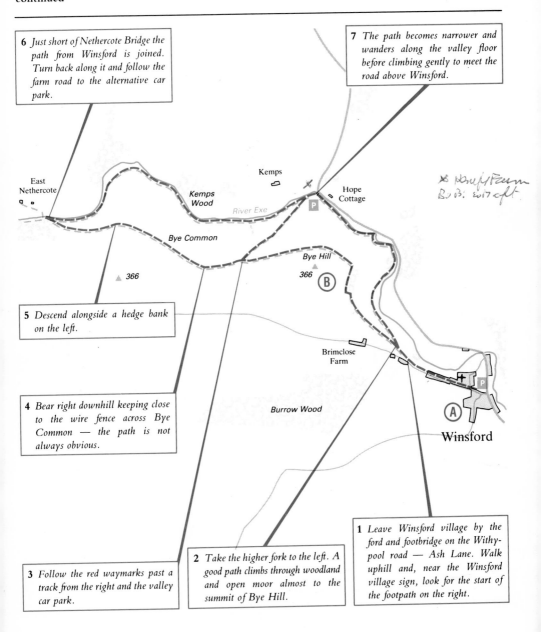

6 Just short of Nethercote Bridge the path from Winsford is joined. Turn back along it and follow the farm road to the alternative car park.

7 The path becomes narrower and wanders along the valley floor before climbing gently to meet the road above Winsford.

East Nethercote

Kemps

Kemps Wood

River Exe

Hope Cottage

Bye Common

Bye Hill

▲ 366

366 ▲ Ⓑ

5 Descend alongside a hedge bank on the left.

Brimclose Farm

Ⓐ

Winsford

4 Bear right downhill keeping close to the wire fence across Bye Common — the path is not always obvious.

Burrow Wood

1 Leave Winsford village by the ford and footbridge on the Withypool road — Ash Lane. Walk uphill and, near the Winsford village sign, look for the start of the footpath on the right.

2 Take the higher fork to the left. A good path climbs through woodland and open moor almost to the summit of Bye Hill.

3 Follow the red waymarks past a track from the right and the valley car park.

29

Walk 14
EXFORD DOWN THE RIVER EXE
5 miles (8 km) Moderate; one steep stretch

This walk contains some of the best scenery that Exmoor has to offer, and could happily occupy a whole day. In spring, the freshness of the beech trees and the carpet of bluebells make it particularly lovely, with the path seeming always to chose the route that gives the best views. The ford above Nethercote is easily crossed in wellington boots, or the adventurous could make use of the two tree trunks spanning the river!

1 *Start from the large car park in Exford opposite the Crown Inn. Leave from the far end and follow the path along the river bank.*

2 *At the second gate opposite the bridge, turn left up a track to a barn. Pass through the gate.*

3 *Do not follow the red marks, but bear right, aiming for the far right-hand corner and two beech trees. Here a path leads down through the bank emerging high above the river.*

4 *Follow the path down to the river and through the gate on to the bank. Cross two stiles into a marshy field and follow the yellow marks to dry land and out on to the lane.*

5 *Keep straight on past Lyncombe Farm and follow the path round Lyncombe Hill.*

6 *EITHER continue along the track to Nethercote, OR along the river bank on a new path.*

7 *Cross by the bridge and immediately turn right through the gate and return to the ford.*

Exford

Court Farm

302

309
Lyncombe
Wood

Road Castle
Earthwork

Court
Copse

Lyncombe

Lyncombe
Hill

River Exe

Road
Hill

Room
Hill

Curr Cleeve

B 3223

381

Ford

West
Nethercote

East
Nethercote

A Exford is a substantial village with two good hostelries and various shops. It is the centre of stag hunting on Exmoor, and it is here that the kennels of the hunt are located.

Over

30

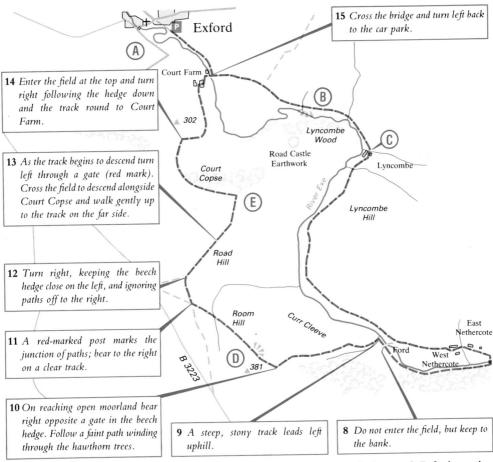

15 *Cross the bridge and turn left back to the car park.*

14 *Enter the field at the top and turn right following the hedge down and the track round to Court Farm.*

13 *As the track begins to descend turn left through a gate (red mark). Cross the field to descend alongside Court Copse and walk gently up to the track on the far side.*

12 *Turn right, keeping the beech hedge close on the left, and ignoring paths off to the right.*

11 *A red-marked post marks the junction of paths; bear to the right on a clear track.*

10 *On reaching open moorland bear right opposite a gate in the beech hedge. Follow a faint path winding through the hawthorn trees.*

9 *A steep, stony track leads left uphill.*

8 *Do not enter the field, but keep to the bank.*

Map labels: Exford, Court Farm, 302, Court Copse, Road Hill, Room Hill, B 3223, 381, Lyncombe Wood, Road Castle Earthwork, River Exe, Lyncombe, Lyncombe Hill, Curr Cleeve, Ford, East Nethercote, West Nethercote

B The steep valley falls away below, with views that are beautiful at any time of the year. Opposite, the earthworks of Road Castle rise above the trees.

C Lyncombe is an interesting old farmhouse, typical of many to be found on Exmoor. Look right down the farm lane to the old hump-backed bridge across the River Exe.

D Room Hill is 1250 feet (381 m) and gives good views over the dramatic Curr Cleeve to Dunkery.

E The scene changes as the track passes through the hedge, and you look towards Exford over the top of Road Castle. This ancient earthwork, which guards the valley of the River Exe, is believed to be an Iron Age fort, although it has also been attributed to the Romans. A small path leads off to the earthworks.

31

LANDACRE TO WITHYPOOL

5 miles (8 km) Moderate; boggy in places

River valleys are always attractive places in which to walk although, by nature, they are bound to be wet in places. This walk is no exception but, with care and proper footwear, there should be no problems. As it broadens, the valley of the River Barle becomes more pastoral with wild moorland giving way to fields, and the farmhouses and cottages becoming more numerous.

Withypool is a popular place, not so much with the day trippers, but with the riders, walkers, and fishermen who know their Exmoor well. There is no room for coaches, so the village escapes the mass invasion that overwhelms neighbouring Winsford.

The church is situated a little way above the village, and will be passed as you leave Withypool. It contains a Norman font.

It is said of the Royal Oak that R D Blackmore wrote much of *Lorna Doone* while staying there. The various owners have avoided the temptation to capitalize on this in any way and it remains an unspoilt country inn.

A Pronounced 'Lanacer', this is a well-known and popular beauty spot. The graceful, five-arched stone bridge is medieval, spanning the Barle as it leaves the moorland and its valley broadens.

B As the path rises, skirting the edge of Withypool Common, the views back down to Landacre and up the Barle valley are very fine. The open moorland rises all around. Close to the summit at 1408 feet (428 m) are the Brightworthy (Brightery) Barrows, ancient burial mounds similar to those found in many places on Exmoor.

C Parking is difficult in Withypool because it clings to the steep valley of the Barle, but one small park has been created near the river. The village lacks an attractive central area because of its steepness, but it has an interesting church and a welcoming inn, the Royal Oak.

Over

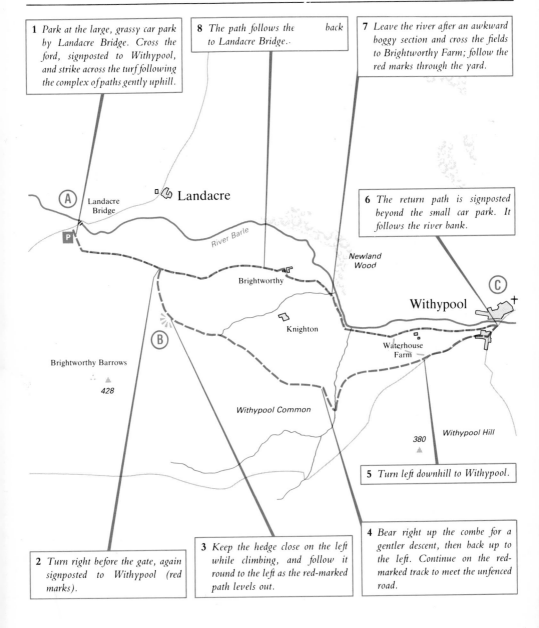

1 Park at the large, grassy car park by Landacre Bridge. Cross the ford, signposted to Withypool, and strike across the turf following the complex of paths gently uphill.

8 The path follows the back to Landacre Bridge.

7 Leave the river after an awkward boggy section and cross the fields to Brightworthy Farm; follow the red marks through the yard.

6 The return path is signposted beyond the small car park. It follows the river bank.

5 Turn left downhill to Withypool.

4 Bear right up the combe for a gentler descent, then back up to the left. Continue on the red-marked track to meet the unfenced road.

3 Keep the hedge close on the left while climbing, and follow it round to the left as the red-marked path levels out.

2 Turn right before the gate, again signposted to Withypool (red marks).

Landacre Bridge

Landacre

River Barle

Brightworthy

Newland Wood

Knighton

Withypool

Waterhouse Farm

Brightworthy Barrows

428

Withypool Common

Withypool Hill

380

Ⓐ Ⓑ Ⓒ P

0 ___ 1 mile
0 ___ 1 km

PORLOCK TO PORLOCK WEIR

$3\frac{1}{2}$ miles ($5\frac{1}{2}$ km) Moderate

The walk starts at bustling Porlock, passes through woodland to reach Porlock Weir, and then returns along the beach. It is quite possible to walk in the reverse direction, but the gradients would be steeper.

Nowadays, Porlock is a tourist village astride the busy main road to Minehead. It is exceedingly picturesque and was a market town in former times. It is still the centre of the local farming community and has a good range of everyday shops, as well as the usual gift shops, cafés, and restaurants. There is also a coffee and tea merchant situated not far from the main car park. The Ship Inn, a former coaching house, is associated with Lorna Doone, as well as with several of the poets who discovered the beauties of Exmoor and the Quantocks before moving north to the Lake District.

The woodland surrounding West Porlock contains stately Spanish chestnuts, beech, and conifers, and the footpath gives glimpses of some beautiful gardens, one of which is open to the public during spring and summer.

Porlock Weir offers refreshment at two inns and a café. It is a most attractive spot and deservedly very popular. Not much evidence is left of the thriving little port that once boasted a fishing fleet and a coastal trade. Before the building of the roads as we know them today, heavy and bulky goods were transported largely by sea, and a port or landing beach was essential. In the nineteenth century, a new jetty was constructed and it was from here that the Knights – who at that time owned the Forest of Exmoor – planned to export the iron and copper from their mines. These did not prove to be as successful as had been hoped, and Porlock Weir gradually declined. Today, it is pleasure craft that lie moored alongside.

A From the shingle beach, the high ridge of Selworthy and Bossington, terminating in Hurlstone Point, can be appreciated, and the tamed, domestic landscape of the vale contrasts with the rugged moorland behind.

B This walk has the added advantage of the possibility of a swim, but the warning notice should be heeded; the shingle shelves steeply and, at low tide, there can be dangerous currents.

Over

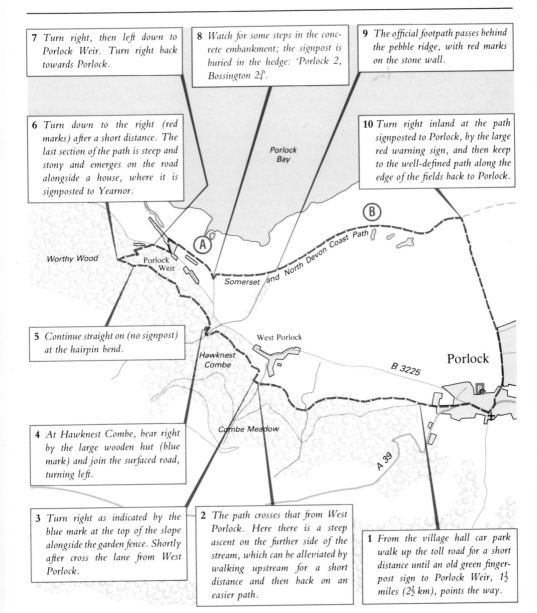

7 Turn right, then left down to Porlock Weir. Turn right back towards Porlock.

8 Watch for some steps in the concrete embankment; the signpost is buried in the hedge: 'Porlock 2, Bossington 2¼'.

9 The official footpath passes behind the pebble ridge, with red marks on the stone wall.

6 Turn down to the right (red marks) after a short distance. The last section of the path is steep and stony and emerges on the road alongside a house, where it is signposted to Yearnor.

10 Turn right inland at the path signposted to Porlock, by the large red warning sign, and then keep to the well-defined path along the edge of the fields back to Porlock.

Porlock Bay

Ⓑ

Worthy Wood

Porlock Weir

Ⓐ

Somerset and North Devon Coast Path

5 Continue straight on (no signpost) at the hairpin bend.

West Porlock

Porlock

B 3225

P

Hawknest Combe

4 At Hawknest Combe, bear right by the large wooden hut (blue mark) and join the surfaced road, turning left.

Combe Meadow

A 39

3 Turn right as indicated by the blue mark at the top of the slope alongside the garden fence. Shortly after cross the lane from West Porlock.

2 The path crosses that from West Porlock. Here there is a steep ascent on the further side of the stream, which can be alleviated by walking upstream for a short distance and then back on an easier path.

1 From the village hall car park walk up the toll road for a short distance until an old green fingerpost sign to Porlock Weir, 1½ miles (2½ km), points the way.

MALMSMEAD

2¼ miles (3½ km) Moderate

At County Gate the Exmoor National Park has a strong presence. A car park with toilets has been provided. From it there are fine views and a panorama board. There is also a memorial to the writer J H B Peel who retired to the Heddon Valley. His *Portrait of Exmoor*, written in 1970, is one man's personal and intimate view of Exmoor, as well as being a reliable guide.

The former gatehouse is now an information centre and shop, selling drinks and light refreshments as well as books, maps, and so on. On the road itself, the two slate gateposts remain although the gates have long since disappeared.

3 Turn sharp left descending to the river bank.

2 Turn left downhill; at this point a path joins from Cosgate Hill car park.

1 Follow the path to the right from the County Gate car park, signposted 'Malmsmead 1½ miles'.

A 39

Cosgate Hill

Ⓐ

Ashton

Ashton Cleave

County Gate

Ⓟ

10 Turn left on the main road back to the car park.

4 Pass in front of Glebe Farm, and continue through a gate along the river bank.

River East Lyn

Glebe Farm

Southern Wood

Ⓒ

9 Go through the gate, signposted 'Malmsmead ¾' and begin the ascent.

5 Cross the river on the humped footbridge, and follow the lane past Parsonage Farm.

Ⓑ Malmsmead

Ogre Water

6 Turn right on the road down to visit Malmsmead.

8 Turn right, then left, following the grassy track between tall hedge banks into the field.

7 Retrace your steps and recross the river.

A The steepness of the scree slopes of Ashton Cleave can be appreciated, and across the valley is the wooded height of Southern Wood.

B Malmsmead is no more than a ford and an old, narrow bridge – or would be were it not for *Lorna Doone*. Here is the start of the tourist path up the Doone Valley, and the accompanying gift shops and cafés.

C The Doone Valley is almost directly opposite with Malmsmead below.

LEY HILL

1 mile (1½ km) Easy

0 ———————————————— 1 mile
0 ———————————————— 1 km

To reach Ley Hill from Porlock, either turn right at the sign to Doverhay, then second right, which is a sharp, uphill turn signposted to Exford and Stoke Pero; or, turn right for Luccombe at Red Post on the Minehead road, and right again, signposted 'Filter Station', then left uphill on the Exford road. The road climbs Crawter Hill. Then, as it levels out, there is an area to the left for car parking, just beyond the trees which are to the right of the road. Even without leaving the car, the views are extremely good.

Both Crawter Hill and Ley Hill form part of the Holnicote Estate, once owned by the Acland family. Many of the paths and rides bear names that recall members of the family, whose home was at Holnicote House, below Selworthy.

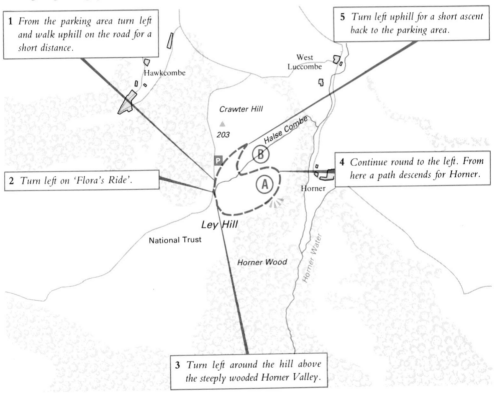

1 *From the parking area turn left and walk uphill on the road for a short distance.*

5 *Turn left uphill for a short ascent back to the parking area.*

West Luccombe

Hawkcombe

Crawter Hill

203

Halse Combe

2 *Turn left on 'Flora's Ride'.*

4 *Continue round to the left. From here a path descends for Horner.*

Horner

Ley Hill

National Trust

Horner Water

Horner Wood

3 *Turn left around the hill above the steeply wooded Horner Valley.*

A A solid stone seat of ample proportions provides an excellent and unusually comfortable base from which to view the surrounding hills and the steep cleft of the Horner Water. The view is towards Horner Hill and Dunkery. The seat is known as the Pentley Seat, and is in memory of Charles Thomas Dyke Acland.

B Halse Combe is the name of this steep valley plunging down to West Horner. Ahead are Bossington and its hill, with Hurlstone Point jutting out into the sea.

WEBBER'S POST TO BROCKWELL

3 miles (5 km) Easy; boggy in places

This route should be appreciated by evening walkers. The time of year will determine the exact location of the setting sun, but the glow on the slopes of Bossington Hill, lighting up Selworthy church, and even setting Porlock Bay on fire, would be sights worth waiting for. This would be a safe walk even in bad weather, although the lower path from Luccombe to Brockwell can be uncomfortably muddy, churned up by the horses that also use this route. There is an escape route by way of short cuts striking right on to the moor.

Luccombe is another of the 'pretty' tourist villages of Exmoor. It may be visited by continuing down hill at Point 3. The village is noted for its thatched cottages and fine church, but there is very limited parking, and the lane is congested in the summer.

A Some car parks are a joy in themselves, and the one at Webber's Post certainly is. Wide grassy areas are surrounded by trees which give rare shade with plenty of room for everyone.

B The pretty village of Luccombe is dominated by its fine church; there is limited parking, but the only visitor facility seems to be the post office.

C Between the trees, there are views across the valley, with the white church of Selworthy prominent beneath the heights of Selworthy Beacon. Wootton Courtenay is the village beneath the afforested slopes of Wootton Common.

D The lower slopes of Dunkery Beacon; from here the moorland rises to the summit without interruptions, but, because of the convex nature of the hill, the summit cannot be seen. Nevertheless, the feeling of having a foothold on a great height is unmistakable. The view extends round to take in Porlock, Bossington, and the Bristol Channel.

Over

0   1 mile

0   1 km

1 *From the car park on the left of the road from Horner to Dunkery, take the track downhill following the edge of the woodland.*

2 *Keep the stream on your right through the woodland descent.*

3 *Turn right and cross the stream via the dam. Pass through tall gates into the forestry plantation.*

4 *Follow the track, slightly downhill, out on to the open moorland, and then sunk between tree-lined banks and areas of woodland.*

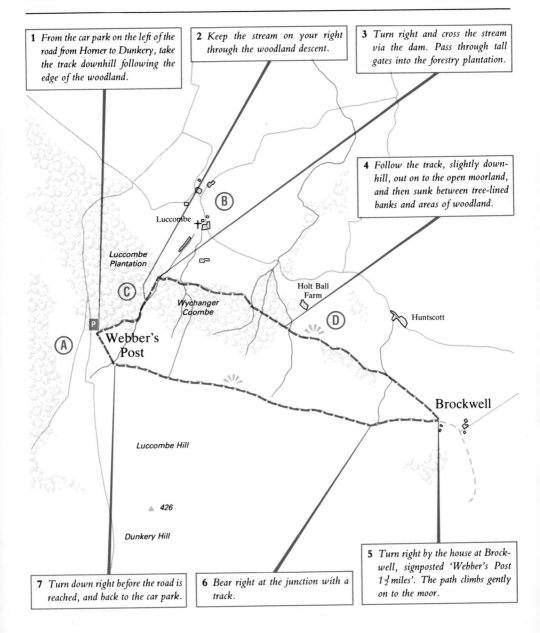

Luccombe

Luccombe
Plantation

Wychanger
Coombe

Holt Ball
Farm

Huntscott

Webber's
Post

Brockwell

Luccombe Hill

▲ 426

Dunkery Hill

5 *Turn right by the house at Brockwell, signposted 'Webber's Post 1½ miles'. The path climbs gently on to the moor.*

7 *Turn down right before the road is reached, and back to the car park.*

6 *Bear right at the junction with a track.*

39

HORNER AND LEY HILL

2 miles (3 km) Moderate; one steep climb

Horner is a delightful village and deservedly popular. The scenery draws many motorists, who take advantage of the tea rooms, and go for a gentle ten-minute stroll along the valley.

There are easy walks in either direction, but the track following the river is the most popular. Many woodland walks, all clearly signposted, start from here, and they are all worth exploring. The woods are rich in wild flowers, birds, and trees, but there are rather too many people for the shy deer.

In the village are two pack-horse bridges of great antiquity, marking Horner's former importance on the route to Dunster.

---

7 Turn right and descend on the Halse Combe side, re-entering the woodlands.

8 Turn right at the bottom on the track back to Horner and the packhorse bridge.

1 Leave the official car park in Horner by the entry road, turn right, then left taking the inconspicuous and unsignposted opening in the hedge that leads to the ancient packhorse bridge across the river.

6 Follow the path round and begin gently to descend, still well above the trees, to reach the seat.

Hawkscombe

Crawter Hill

▲ 203

Halse Combe

Packhorse Bridge

P

Horner

B C A

Ley Hill

5 Fork right, above the tree line and the path levels out.

Rey Combe

Horner Water

Horner Wood

Horner Hill

2 Turn slightly right, then left uphill following the gently graded path up Rey Combe.

3 At a junction, turn right and continue uphill.

4 Walk straight on at the junction.

A The car park at Horner is provided with toilets and an information board, but it is not large and parking space is at a premium.

B Deviate slightly uphill to the highest point. The views extend over Porlock and Porlock Bay to the Welsh coast, as well as to Bossington and Selworthy.

C The large stone seat in memory of Thomas Charles Acland provides a marvellous vantage point overlooking the former Acland lands of Horner and the Holnicote Estate, given to the National Trust in 1944.

HORNER HILL

2½ miles (4 km) Moderate; one steep climb

Horner Hill dominates the small hamlet of Horner below and, from all angles, it appears intimidatingly steep. Driving up to the car park seems the only easy route but, whichever way you leave

Webber's Post, a steep drop is inevitable.

Horner Hill is criss-crossed with paths and tracks, most with names commemorating members of the Acland family.

The Judge's Path is the one easy way back up to the summit. It keeps to the trees, so there are no views, but the woodland is quite beautiful enough in its own right.

3 *Turn left at the junction and go straight down to the road.*

4 *Turn left down to Horner. Retrace your steps and leave the road at the same point.*

5 *Follow the track, bearing left. Ignore the left-hand track to Chapel Cross. Continue on the easily graded track to the road.*

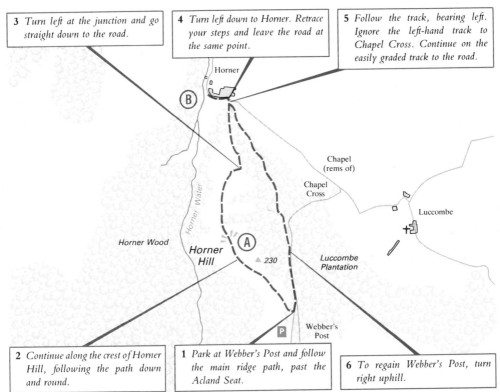

2 *Continue along the crest of Horner Hill, following the path down and round.*

1 *Park at Webber's Post and follow the main ridge path, past the Acland Seat.*

6 *To regain Webber's Post, turn right uphill.*

A The main path passes the Acland seat on which is inscribed: 'A lease for 500 years of 8400 acres at Horner, North Hill and Winsford was granted in 1919 to the National Trust by Sir Thomas Acland, his brother and nephew, to secure to the public the enjoy-

ment of the beauty of these hills and moors and the preservation of their natural features'.

The views include the whole panorama of the Horner valley, Cloutsham, Bossington, Selworthy, and Porlock Bay; Dunkery blocks the view magnificently in

the other direction.

B Horner is a small and popular hamlet with the lure of refreshments, but no inn. The walk could be done in reverse but parking is easier at Webber's Post.

WEBBER'S POST TO STOKE PERO
5 miles (8 km) Moderate; one steep climb

0   1 mile

0   1 km

Parking is permitted over a large area at Webber's Post which is beautifully sited and the start of many well-marked walks. It is one of the most popular spots on the whole moor. Tom Webber was a well-known hunting character who died in 1863. It was said of him that he was always in the field and ever at his post. He is buried at King's Brompton.

9 *Beyond the hedge aim for the thorn tree from where the gate into the woods is obvious. For Stoke Pero continue on the path to come out below the church. Retrace your steps and follow the path into the woods, signposted Horner and Webber's Post.*

2 *Turn left downhill on a narrow path that descends steeply.*

3 *Turn left by the National Trust stone collecting box down to the stream. Cross on the footbridge.*

1 *From Webber's Post, leave by the main path to the right.*

Luccombe Plantation

Horner Wood

Stoke Wood

Ⓒ

Webber's Post

Stoke Pero

Cloutsham Ball

Ⓐ

272

Cloutsham

8 *At Cloutsham Farm the path goes through a gate, right down the track, and then left through a gate into the fields. Again, follow the hedge on the left.*

Ⓑ

East Water

4 *Turn right up the hill. The path climbs through oak woodlands.*

7 *At the junction, take the higher, left-hand path. Keep to the high ground climbing gently through some pine trees, past a bench.*

6 *Bear right uphill.*

5 *Bear left at the top following the Nature Trail sign, to emerge in the open on Cloutsham Ball 850 feet (260 m).*

Over

0   1 mile

0   1 km

11 *Pass the second footbridge; take either the track or the path along the river bank (they reunite further down).*

12 *Cross the river on the next footbridge, signposted to Cloutsham and Dunkery.*

13 *Cross the second footbridge and, at the junction, leave the river and start to climb uphill.*

10 *Cross the footbridge at the bottom and bear right, following the river.*

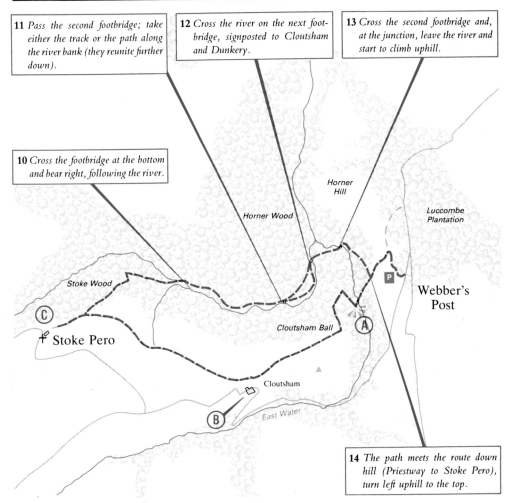

Horner Hill

Horner Wood

Luccombe Plantation

Stoke Wood

(C)

✝ Stoke Pero

Webber's Post

P

Cloutsham Ball

(A)

Cloutsham

(B)

East Water

14 *The path meets the route down hill (Priestway to Stoke Pero), turn left uphill to the top.*

A By deviating to the left, you come out of the woods to get fine views back across the deep valley to Horner, and ahead to the bulk of Dunkery.

B Cloutsham was built originally by the Acland family as a hunting lodge, and is now an imposing farmhouse, only the back of which is to be seen on this walk.

C Stoke Pero's tiny church is set in so deep a hollow that the tower does not rise above the surrounding land. Although it has been much restored, this simple church is interesting and restful. Once, its isolated situation made it popular with those wishing to marry out of sight of inquisitive eyes.

43

BOSSINGTON HILL

4 miles (6½ km) Moderate; one steep climb

The bulk of Bossington Hill appears much higher than it really is. It rises almost sheer from the Vale of Porlock, dominating this sheltered and fertile area. Strong walkers will want to continue to the greater height of Selworthy Beacon, following the well-worn ridge path.

There is a road along the top, reached only from Minehead. This means that Selworthy Beacon is too easily accessible; Bossington remains much less visited. The area is now owned by the National Trust. It was part of the Holnicote Estate owned by the Acland family.

The walk has no problems except for the short haul up to the summit, but it should be noted that the path around the slope of Bossington Hill is narrow, with the land falling sharply, and sufferers from vertigo will find it unpleasant.

A Lynch is a pleasant hamlet with some lovely old houses. The farm now holds a comprehensive agricultural museum with working animals and rare breeds, as well as an unspoilt sixteenth-century chapel.

B The views from Church Combe are over Porlock Bay and the village of Bossington.

C The summit of Bossington Hill, at 850 feet (259 m), is marked by a large cairn. As a viewpoint it is magnificent with only the greater height of Selworthy Beacon blocking a 360-degree panorama. As with all this area of Exmoor, Dunkery dominates the inland vista, but the Vale of Porlock is laid out beneath with the blue of Porlock Bay, Culbone Hill, and the deep combes of Horner adding interest.

The Welsh coast and mountains are also visible - sometimes! But there would be little point in climbing Bossington Hill on anything but a clear day.

Over

44

0   1 mile

0   1 km

4 *At the second crossing of paths, turn left, signposted to Hurlstone Point. The path runs gently uphill through woodland and suddenly comes out into the open.*

5 *At the junction with the steep path from Hurlstone Combe, turn right – not on the coast path to Minehead.*

6 *Turn right for the summit of Bossington Hill, then retrace your steps to the junction and turn right.*

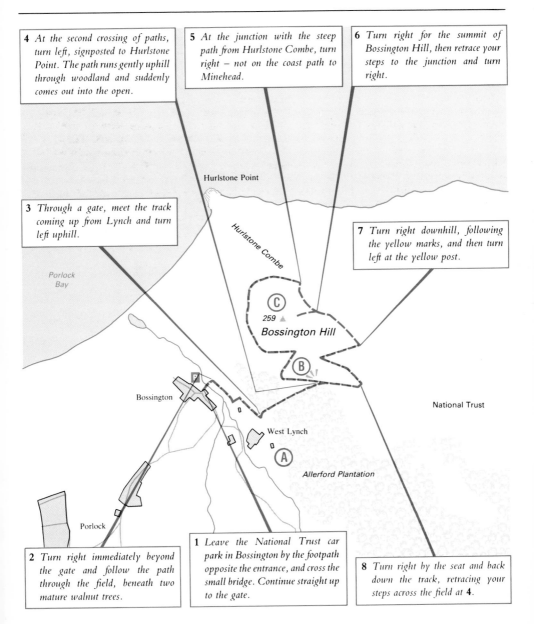

Hurlstone Point

3 *Through a gate, meet the track coming up from Lynch and turn left uphill.*

7 *Turn right downhill, following the yellow marks, and then turn left at the yellow post.*

Hurlstone Combe

Porlock Bay

Ⓒ

259 ▲

Bossington Hill

Ⓑ

National Trust

Bossington

West Lynch

Ⓐ

Allerford Plantation

Porlock

2 *Turn right immediately beyond the gate and follow the path through the field, beneath two mature walnut trees.*

1 *Leave the National Trust car park in Bossington by the footpath opposite the entrance, and cross the small bridge. Continue straight up to the gate.*

8 *Turn right by the seat and back down the track, retracing your steps across the field at* **4**.

DUNSTER PARK, GALLAX HILL, AND BAT'S CASTLE

4½ miles (7¼ km) Moderate

Dunster is a small town full of history and lovely buildings. It well repays exploration and, apart from Dunster Castle, there are the fine church containing monuments to the Luttrell family, a restored water mill, the picturesque yarn or buttermarket built in 1609, and the Luttrell Arms, once the residence of the Abbots of Cleeve.

In its early history, Dunster was a busy port and, latterly, the market town for the eastern area of Exmoor and the Brendons. Although it caters largely for the tourists it has, remarkably, retained its character intact.

The name of Luttrell is synonymous with this part of Exmoor and, until 1950, the family owned Dunster itself. The castle has been their home since 1376, and there was originally a Norman fortress on the same site. It saw action during the Civil War as a result of which parts of it were dismantled. Much of it was rebuilt and res-

tored in the 1870s. It is now owned by the National Trust.

The gardens are also very fine and here, as elsewhere in the town, the mild climate ensures luxuriant growth.

During the season, parking in Dunster is difficult. The walk starts from a small and poorly signposted car park at the inland end of the town reached via the lane between the Foresters Arms and the telephone box.

A Gallax Bridge crosses the River Avill alongside a ford. It takes its name from Gallax Hill above. It is an ancient packhorse bridge, of which there are few surviving examples on Exmoor. Strings of small horses or ponies were almost the only method of transportation over hilly terrain with few roads. Many of the deeply sunken, stony lanes that cross the valleys were part of the packhorse network. A laden horse, carrying bulging panniers on either side, travelling in strings of up to a dozen, was a hazard to be avoided.

B From Black Ball there is a viewpoint through a break in the trees. Across the valley of the River Avill rises the height of Grabbist Hill, dominating Dunster. This is the eastern end of a high ridge running from Wootton Courtenay, much of which is now forested.

C Bat's Castle is an Iron Age fort occupying a splendid position. Because it is situated in moorland, it has escaped damage from farm vehicles and has survived in an excellent state of preservation. At 692 feet (210 m), it commands the coastal plain, and a gentle walk around the perimeter will give a

360-degree scenic display that is hard to beat.

D Gallax Hill was reputedly originally Gallows Hill – a windy spot on which to meet one's end, although the last earthly view would be a good one!

From both airy eminences, the views are panoramic. The Quantocks lie to the east, the Welsh coast and the Welsh mountains are clear across the Bristol Channel, as is much of the Channel coast of Somerset. The heights of Selworthy and Dunkery dominate the western and south-western arc with the wooded slopes of Croydon Hill and the Brendons to the south-east.

Over

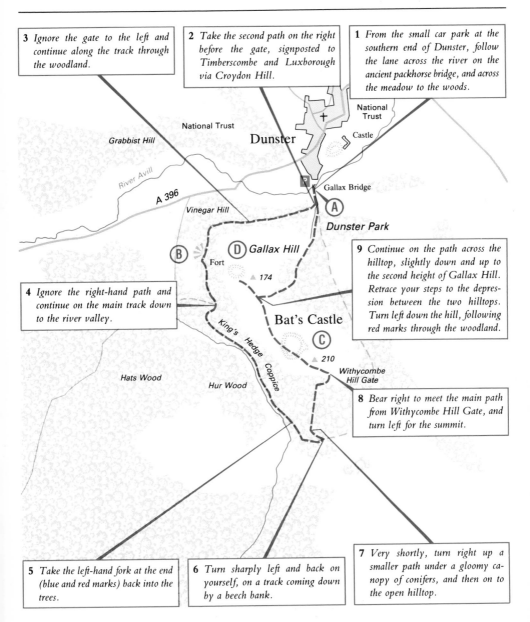

3 Ignore the gate to the left and continue along the track through the woodland.

2 Take the second path on the right before the gate, signposted to Timberscombe and Luxborough via Croydon Hill.

1 From the small car park at the southern end of Dunster, follow the lane across the river on the ancient packhorse bridge, and across the meadow to the woods.

National Trust

Grabbist Hill

National Trust

Dunster

Castle

National Trust

River Avill

A 396

Gallax Bridge

Vinegar Hill

(A)

Dunster Park

(B)

(D) Gallax Hill

Fort

▲ 174

9 Continue on the path across the hilltop, slightly down and up to the second height of Gallax Hill. Retrace your steps to the depression between the two hilltops. Turn left down the hill, following red marks through the woodland.

4 Ignore the right-hand path and continue on the main track down to the river valley.

King's Hedge Coppice

Bat's Castle

(C)

▲ 210

Hats Wood

Hur Wood

Withycombe Hill Gate

8 Bear right to meet the main path from Withycombe Hill Gate, and turn left for the summit.

5 Take the left-hand fork at the end (blue and red marks) back into the trees.

6 Turn sharply left and back on yourself, on a track coming down by a beech bank.

7 Very shortly, turn right up a smaller path under a gloomy canopy of conifers, and then on to the open hilltop.

47

BOSSINGTON TO HURLSTONE POINT
2¼ miles (3½ km) Easy

This walk could be dedicated to non-walkers who have decided to try walking. The furthest point would not be too far to carry a picnic and idle away an afternoon.

More energetic walkers could ascend Bossington Hill (*see* Walk 23).

Bossington is a famed Exmoor beauty spot, well known for its walnut trees, and for its several tea gardens. There is a track to the beach at Porlock Bay and, a short distance inland at Lynch, is the West Somerset farm museum.

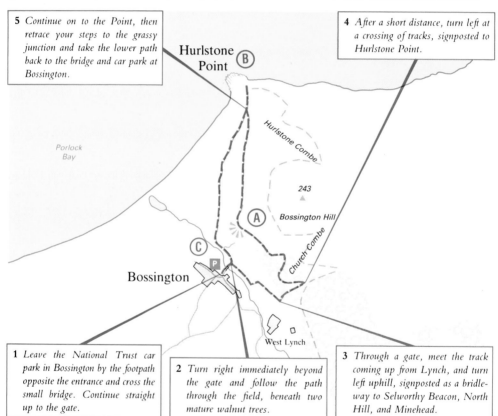

5 *Continue on to the Point, then retrace your steps to the grassy junction and take the lower path back to the bridge and car park at Bossington.*

4 *After a short distance, turn left at a crossing of tracks, signposted to Hurlstone Point.*

Hurlstone Point Ⓑ

Hurlstone Combe

Porlock Bay

243 ▲

Ⓐ *Bossington Hill*

Church Combe

Ⓒ

🅿

Bossington

West Lynch

1 *Leave the National Trust car park in Bossington by the footpath opposite the entrance and cross the small bridge. Continue straight up to the gate.*

2 *Turn right immediately beyond the gate and follow the path through the field, beneath two mature walnut trees.*

3 *Through a gate, meet the track coming up from Lynch, and turn left uphill, signposted as a bridle-way to Selworthy Beacon, North Hill, and Minehead.*

A There is a fine view over the whole of Porlock Bay. The lush vale and the village of Porlock can be seen behind, and there is Dunkery inland.

B Hurlstone Point is a rocky promontory with a coastguard lookout and a safe, concrete platform from which to admire the view. The prominent notice board warns that the path is dangerous, but it refers to the section beyond the lookout.

C The cottages of Bossington are all attractive with rounded chimneys, thatch, and lovely gardens. Walnut trees are a feature, and the village is renowned for its cream teas.

TIMBERSCOMBE COMMON

2½ miles (3½ km) Easy

Timberscombe is one of the quieter villages of the Brendons although it does have to bear the summer traffic rushing through to Dunster and the coast.

It has some fine old houses particularly around the Rock Inn,

a former coaching house. The church is worth a visit; it is largely fifteenth century with a massive entrance door. The unusually shaped spire is a Queen Anne addition.

A visit to the village can easily be included by turning downhill by the quarry at Point **4**, and climbing straight up between the houses to rejoin the walk at Point **6**.

5 Turn immediately right, uphill slightly, to join the track by the silver birches.

6 Follow the track through the trees and through a yellow-marked gate at the top.

7 Cross the field, following the electricity poles, keeping the wood to your right, and enter the woods through a yellow-marked gate.

Timberscombe

Ⓑ

Timberscombe Common

4 Continue along the contour passing through a gate, and follow the hedge down to a red-marked small gate.

8 Turn right through a break in the bank on to the main track along the forest perimeter, and then left back to the car.

Broadwood Plantation

Timberscombe Wood

Ⓐ

Ⓟ

1 Park in the wide area created by the Forestry Commission at their twin entrances just above the 'Steep Hill' sign on the main road from Dunster to Luxborough. Pass through the gate (red mark) going downhill on a broad drive and past a fire tower.

3 Pass through the small gate and immediately turn right through a second gate. Contour above the valley towards Timberscombe.

2 Cross the perimeter track and go through a gate into a field. Follow the farm track down to the gate.

A As you emerge from the woodland, Dunkery dominates the view ahead, bare headed and gaunt, in contrast to the nearer,

afforested hills of Tivington and Wootton Common and of Croydon Hill.

B There are fine views across the Avill valley to the steep slopes.

SLOWLEY WOOD AND WITHYCOMBE COMMON

3 miles (5 km) Easy

The deep valleys of Luxborough and the Washford River separate Withycombe and Rodhuish Commons from the Brendons. Few people pass this way, and the inn at Luxborough is the only source of refreshment.

The hamlet's church is situated a mile (1½ km) or so away up the valley at Churchtown. There are plenty of walks on all sides, but there is nowhere to leave a car on the narrow country lanes. Withycombe Common is 1252 feet (382 m) above sea level and the archeologists will find interest in the cairns and tumuli to the south of the trig point.

A Until comparatively recently, some Forestry Commission walks have been oppressive with dense, dark woodland all around and no views. But Slowley Wood is pleasant. The trees are mature and the forest tracks are broad. Here the trees have been felled (not recently) and the valley opens up ahead giving views across the hamlet of Luxborough towards the ridge that is the spine of the Brendon Hills, with the line of trees marking the road.

B Make a short deviation here on the Perley Barn path to look down Perley Combe to Churchtown – a steep valley surrounded by woods.

C Withycombe Common is a magnificent viewpoint with many comfortable heathery seats from which to admire it. The Welsh coast is clear; the heights of Selworthy Beacon and Bossington Hill dominate the left, and the Quantocks bar the view to the right with Washford and Williton in the vale between.

D As the path drops down, the views inland open out, again towards the spine of the Brendons. The moorland has all but disappeared, and it is a largely agricultural landscape, with deeply wooded combes.

Over

0   0   1 mile
0   1 km

6 *Six routes converge here and care is needed. Do not take the blue-marked path signposted to Dunster, but the second (unmarked) path on the right which quickly leads to the trig point on Withycombe Common.*

7 *Turn right where the main track bears left and follow the track back along the edge of the forest.*

8 *Pass through the gate into a field (no marks). The official path crosses the middle of the field to the corresponding gate.*

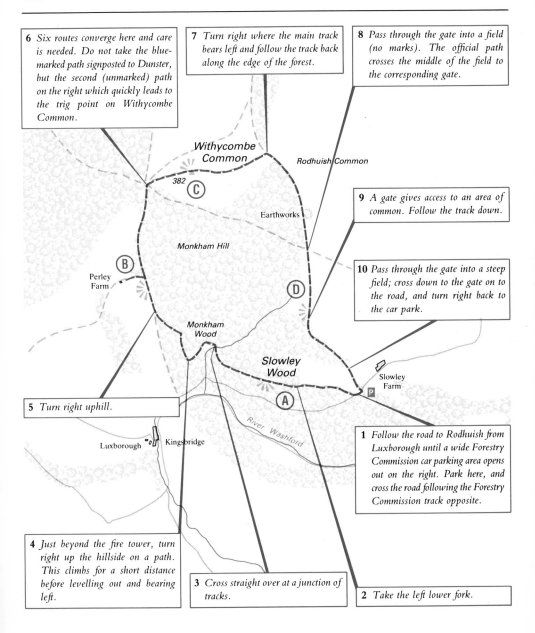

Withycombe Common

Rodhuish Common

382 Ⓒ

Earthworks

9 *A gate gives access to an area of common. Follow the track down.*

Monkham Hill

Ⓑ

Perley Farm

Ⓓ

10 *Pass through the gate into a steep field; cross down to the gate on to the road, and turn right back to the car park.*

Monkham Wood

Slowley Wood

Ⓐ

Slowley Farm

5 *Turn right uphill.*

Luxborough Kingsbridge

River Washford

1 *Follow the road to Rodhuish from Luxborough until a wide Forestry Commission car parking area opens out on the right. Park here, and cross the road following the Forestry Commission track opposite.*

4 *Just beyond the fire tower, turn right up the hillside on a path. This climbs for a short distance before levelling out and bearing left.*

3 *Cross straight over at a junction of tracks.*

2 *Take the left lower fork.*

51

THE BRENDONS: HADDON HILL AND WIMBLEBALL RESERVOIR
2¾ miles (4½ km) Moderate

Haddon Hill has always been an attractive place – open and airy with good all-round views. Below, the River Haddeo winds in its steep, wooded valley down to the hamlet of Bury.

Some would claim that the construction in 1974–80 of Wimbleball Reservoir ruined the scenery; others feel that the large expanse of water only enhances the view. The River Haddeo has been tamed and harnessed and, by drowning two valleys, an irregularly shaped lake has been created, with further car parks, picnic areas, and an information centre at Cowlings and Bessom Bridge.

Haddon Hill itself is good walking country with a gentle uphill climb leading to the summit. From here, the track continues, and several variations lead down through the woodland.

Recent forestry operations have disrupted the ground and some of the tracks, and there is no way across the river between Bury and Hartford, although it is fordable in wellington boots.

The car park at Frogwell Lodge is well placed although a perimeter bank prevents views from most of the parking area itself.

A From the summit of Haddon Hill, 1163 feet (354 m), there are extensive views in all directions. Dartmoor's outline looms across the broad expanse of rural Devon. The Blackdown Hills and the Wellington Monument can be seen across the flat lands of Somerset with Dunkery and Exmoor close by. Below is the sparkling expanse of the reservoir with the village of Brompton Regis to the left.

B The dam is 160 feet (49 m) high, blocking the Haddeo river which, far below, resumes its course. The dam may be crossed.

C Through the woods are several paths that once crossed the valley to Upton or West Hill; now they are overgrown through disuse. The woods are part of a former deer park.

Across the valley is Upton Farm and the ruined tower of the former parish church. Although restored in 1796, it was abandoned in 1867 when a new church was built on the roadside. The norman font and three bells were transferred from the original church, which was small, only 66 feet (20 m) long by 13 feet (4 m) wide, and dated from the mid-fourteenth century. Now, only the tower remains in the middle of a field.

Over

0   1 mile

0   1 km

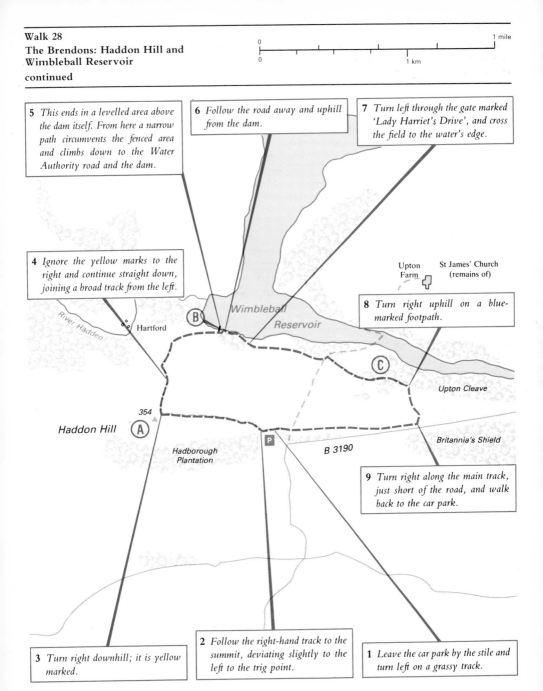

5 *This ends in a levelled area above the dam itself. From here a narrow path circumvents the fenced area and climbs down to the Water Authority road and the dam.*

6 *Follow the road away and uphill from the dam.*

7 *Turn left through the gate marked 'Lady Harriet's Drive', and cross the field to the water's edge.*

4 *Ignore the yellow marks to the right and continue straight down, joining a broad track from the left.*

Upton Farm   St James' Church (remains of)

8 *Turn right uphill on a blue-marked footpath.*

River Haddeo   Hartford

Ⓑ   *Wimbleball Reservoir*

Ⓒ

Upton Cleave

354

Haddon Hill   Ⓐ

Hadborough Plantation

Ⓟ

B 3190

Britannia's Shield

9 *Turn right along the main track, just short of the road, and walk back to the car park.*

3 *Turn right downhill; it is yellow marked.*

2 *Follow the right-hand track to the summit, deviating slightly to the left to the trig point.*

1 *Leave the car park by the stile and turn left on a grassy track.*

THE BRENDONS: LYPE HILL

6 miles (8 km) Moderate; wet by stream

Lype Hill at 1390 feet (423 m) is the highest point of the Brendons. It is an unrivalled viewpoint, yet it is seldom visited and there are no signposts or car parks on the main road.

The walk from Cutcombe is one for explorers. It is not hard to find but few walkers pass this way. A yellow-marked track follows the right-hand bank from Putham Ford but is not to be preferred because it passes through a forested area.

1 *From the parking area by the church in Cutcombe, take the first gate to the left on the opposite side of the lane. Cross the field diagonally to a small stile in the left-hand corner.*

2 *Walk diagonally downwards to a gate and continue downwards, aiming for a gap in the river bank trees where there is one prominent tree.*

3 *Follow the overgrown track down to the water's edge.*

4 *A ruined building, half hidden in undergrowth, stands in the water; the path passes in front and behind it and turns back upstream. It then bears left through the trees.*

5 *At Putham Ford, cross the stream and follow the road uphill.*

6 *Take the track on the right across the fields.*

7 *Pass through open woodland and take the gate that leads down to the stream.*

8 *Cross the stream and aim for the gap in the beech bank. Turn left following the line of beech trees.*

Ⓐ
🅿 +
Cutcombe
Golden Cleeve Wood
Ⓑ
Kersham
Putham
Putham Ford
Kersham Hill
Highley Plantation
Pitleigh
Ⓒ
B 3224
Hart Cleeve
Lype Hill
423 Ⓓ

A Cutcombe village is usually by-passed. The lane goes nowhere but to the church and a few cottages, and most people stay at Wheddon Cross. The church is somewhat overrestored inside, but it has two fine gargoyles on the tower and occupies a pleasant site above the valley.

Over

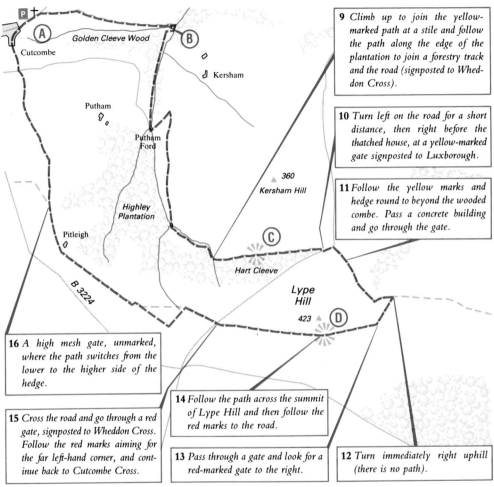

9 *Climb up to join the yellow-marked path at a stile and follow the path along the edge of the plantation to join a forestry track and the road (signposted to Wheddon Cross).*

10 *Turn left on the road for a short distance, then right before the thatched house, at a yellow-marked gate signposted to Luxborough.*

11 *Follow the yellow marks and hedge round to beyond the wooded combe. Pass a concrete building and go through the gate.*

16 *A high mesh gate, unmarked, where the path switches from the lower to the higher side of the hedge.*

14 *Follow the path across the summit of Lype Hill and then follow the red marks to the road.*

15 *Cross the road and go through a red gate, signposted to Wheddon Cross. Follow the red marks aiming for the far left-hand corner, and continue back to Cutcombe Cross.*

13 *Pass through a gate and look for a red-marked gate to the right.*

12 *Turn immediately right uphill (there is no path).*

B Hidden amid the dense undergrowth are quite extensive ruins. This is the site of Stowey Mill, now long disused, but the reason for the many paths that converge here from all directions.

C As the path rises, there are surprising views. Ahead is the bulk of Bossington and Selworthy with Dunkery to the left, and glimpses of the Bristol Channel to the right.

D The view is extraordinary, not least because it is unexpected. The eye travels in an arc over most of Devon as far as Dartmoor, across to the heights of Somerset, over Bossington and Selworthy to the Bristol Channel and Wales, and to Dunkery, the only point higher than the summit of Lype Common.

55

QUANTOCKS: BEACON HILL AND HODDER'S COMBE

5 miles (8 km) Moderate; wet in places

The walk to Beacon Hill is not much more than a simple stroll. Nevertheless, if time is short, it is worthwhile, but far more rewarding is the extended walk leading on and down to Holford's Combe. Both start from the magnificently sited car park, which is not signposted, in keeping with the Quantocks' secretive nature.

Take the lane from West Quantoxhead opposite Staple Lane. This climbs up and up, then levels out, passing through woodland, with wide grassy verges offering many car parking places. The views from the terminal area are good – an excellent place to leave the car-bound.

Rhododendrons add vibrant colour to the woodland in early summer and a haze of bluebells spreads down the combes.

It is not necessary to descend to Vinny Combe, but the climb up is gentle and offers variety to what would otherwise be a moorland walk, especially so if Hodder's Combe is not included and the walk is ended at Beacon Hill.

The site of Beacon Hill, at the north-west extremity of the Quantocks before they drop to the Bristol Channel, meant that it was an excellent place for a fire beacon, one of the many that formed a warning chain along the coast.

Hodder's Combe is a typical Quantocks combe; silent, still, undisturbed except by the little stream, with dappled woodland and a mass of wortleberries.

The path around Lady's Edge climbs gently, emerging suddenly from the wood on to the open moorland. The walk could be extended by continuing down from Longstone Hill to Holford for lunch and back up the combe.

A Williton is the small town in the middle distance, and sometimes a plume of smoke betrays the presence of a West Somerset steam train on the line from Taunton to Minehead. The coast at Minehead can be seen, with Bratton Ball behind.

B Beacon Hill is an excellent viewpoint. At 1019 feet (310 m), it commands a panorama limited only by your eyesight – or a haze. The Welsh coast can seem very close, with the mountains behind, and it is interesting to look across to Exmoor and the Brendon Hills. The Quantocks lie all around with enticing tracks in all directions.

Hinkley Point Power Station has marred the coastline to the east since 1957. The buildings seem large even at this distance; each reactor building is 180 feet (55 m) high, 345 feet (105 m) long, and 185 feet (56 m) wide. The power station makes extensive use of the waters of the Bristol Channel.

C As one descends Longstone Hill the views eastwards are over Bridgwater and the Somerset levels to the Mendips. On a clear day, Glastonbury Tor and Brent Knoll stand out above the flat lands of western Somerset.

Over

0   1 mile

0   1 km

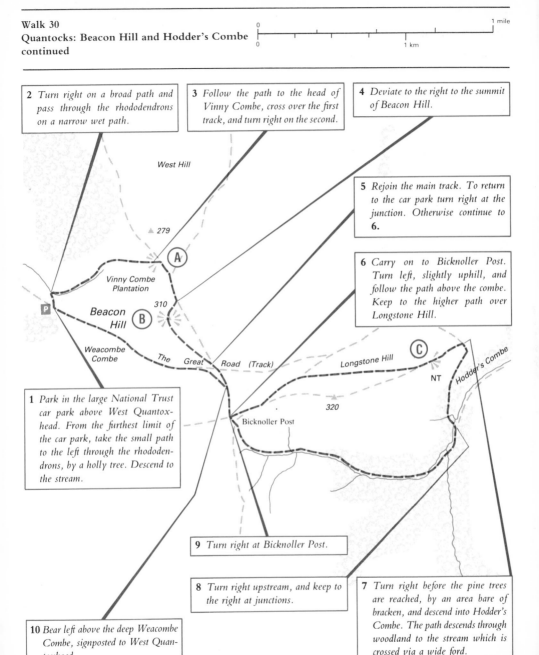

2 *Turn right on a broad path and pass through the rhododendrons on a narrow wet path.*

3 *Follow the path to the head of Vinny Combe, cross over the first track, and turn right on the second.*

4 *Deviate to the right to the summit of Beacon Hill.*

West Hill

5 *Rejoin the main track. To return to the car park turn right at the junction. Otherwise continue to* **6.**

▲ 279

Ⓐ

Vinny Combe
Plantation

6 *Carry on to Bicknoller Post. Turn left, slightly uphill, and follow the path above the combe. Keep to the higher path over Longstone Hill.*

310

Beacon Hill Ⓑ

Ⓟ

Weacombe
Combe   The   Great   Road   (Track)   Longstone Hill   Ⓒ   Hodder's Combe

NT

1 *Park in the large National Trust car park above West Quantoxhead. From the furthest limit of the car park, take the small path to the left through the rhododendrons, by a holly tree. Descend to the stream.*

320

Bicknoller Post

9 *Turn right at Bicknoller Post.*

8 *Turn right upstream, and keep to the right at junctions.*

7 *Turn right before the pine trees are reached, by an area bare of bracken, and descend into Hodder's Combe. The path descends through woodland to the stream which is crossed via a wide ford.*

10 *Bear left above the deep Weacombe Combe, signposted to West Quantoxhead.*

57

QUANTOCKS: WILL'S NECK

7 miles (11 km) Moderate

A climb to the summit of Will's Neck is a must for all serious explorers of the Quantock Hills. It is the highest point, and provides extensive views over the southern and western arcs. The quiet, rural beauty of the scene is currently marred by quarrying operations above Triscombe. Indeed, if much more of the rich red hillside is excavated, poor old Will could find his throat cut!

There are three possible starting points for this walk. From Crowcombe Gate gives the longest walk with the advantage of a mile (1½ km) or so along the ridge of the Quantocks. The car park by the Triscombe Stone is within easy striking distance of the summit; or the car could be left at Triscombe, although there is no official car park. Triscombe does, however, boast an attractive old inn, The Blue Ball, situated at the crossroads of the lanes to West Bagborough and the quarries.

A Views from this hill, a former fire beacon site, are across the plain with the villages of Stogumber, Monksilver, Lydeard St Lawrence, and, immediately below, Crowcombe. The land rises to the Brendons and Exmoor.

B There are some particularly fine trees in these woods – sweet chestnuts lower down, and lime trees on the right as you climb. Close to the summit, you walk on a raised causeway between deep ditches of unknown origin or purpose.

C Will's Neck, at 1260 feet (383 m), is the highest point on the Quantocks. Its summit has an ancient cairn and a fire signal pit. The views from the summit and from the left-hand track are superb.

D The Triscombe Stone is easily missed. It is in the alternative car park for the walk, and this car park can only be approached from the east. The Stone's origins are obscure but it was associated with the Devil and was avoided at night.

Over

1 *Park at Crowcombe Gate and go through the gate on the lower side of the grid.*

12 *The path becomes a broad track between trees, a straight line back to Crowcombe Gate.*

11 *Bear right and downhill; from here the car park is in sight.*

2 *Bear right on the track across the field. Descend into Little Quantock Combe and turn right downhill.*

3 *Before the farm gate, turn left on to a path leading uphill.*

4 *Go through the gate into the woods.*

5 *Turn downhill in Triscombe Combe.*

6 *Turn left on the lane, then right beyond the Blue Ball Inn, signposted to Bagborough.*

7 *Keep left on the track as the lane bends away right.*

8 *Join a path coming from the right and climb gently.*

9 *By a dry pond, turn left across open moorland and keep to the right-hand track.*

10 *Take the left-hand track.*

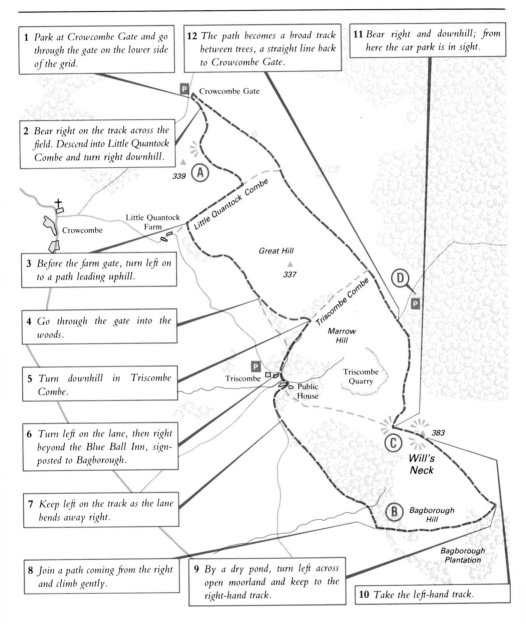

P Crowcombe Gate

339 Ⓐ

Little Quantock Combe

Little Quantock Farm

Crowcombe

Great Hill
337

Triscombe Combe

Ⓓ
P

Marrow Hill

P Triscombe

Public House

Triscombe Quarry

383
Ⓒ
Will's Neck

Ⓑ Bagborough Hill

Bagborough Plantation

QUANTOCKS: BLACK HILL AND HOLFORD COMBE

4 miles (6½ km) Moderate; wet in places

With so many airy possibilities from which to choose, it is difficult to recommend one walk rather than another, or one combe in favour of another. But this route offers views over north and south Somerset, and beyond. It has a choice of starting points, and combines some of the best upland tracks with a very lovely combe.

Parking at the end of the track from Holford is limited, but shady. Most people will prefer the high-level car parks off the road from Crowcombe to Nether Stowey. Shade is available at Crowcombe Combe Gate immediately beyond the cattle grid, or there are two alternatives reached by tracks off the road to the left, a little further on, neither of which is signposted.

The walk could be extended down into Holford, another pretty Quantocks village with an inn. It is associated with the Wordsworths who stayed at Alfoxton Park, now a hotel, and happily rambled over these hills.

A This unnamed summit commands a 360-degree view. From here you can see the lowlands of Somerset, as well as the Blackdown Hills with the Wellington Monument, a landmark for miles around. The valley between the Quantocks and the Brendons lies below. All around, the Quantock uplands offer tempting possibilities to the walker, Nearby is the wooded height of Robin Upright's Hill and the earthworks of Dowsborough Fort.

B A few cairns and hummocks mark the lower summit of Higher Hare Knap but, from here, on a clear day, the view seems limitless. It extends not only over the Bristol Channel to the Welsh coast and mountains but northwards over most of Somerset including the Mendip Hills, to the Malverns and the Brecon Beacons. Bridgwater Bay and Weston-super-Mare, with the twin islands of Flat Holme and Steep Holme as well as the port of Watchet, are closer to hand.

C The confluence of several streams at the junction of Holford Combe with Lady's and Frog Combe is a delightful grassy glade of sylvan beauty – a place for lingering before beginning the gentle climb.

Over

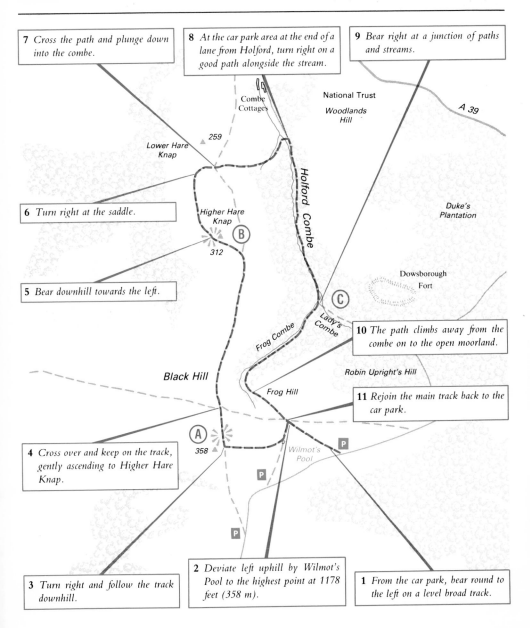

7 *Cross the path and plunge down into the combe.*

8 *At the car park area at the end of a lane from Holford, turn right on a good path alongside the stream.*

9 *Bear right at a junction of paths and streams.*

National Trust

Combe Cottages

Woodlands Hill

A 39

259

Lower Hare Knap

Holford Combe

Duke's Plantation

6 *Turn right at the saddle.*

Higher Hare Knap

B

312

Dowsborough Fort

C

5 *Bear downhill towards the left.*

Lady's Combe

10 *The path climbs away from the combe on to the open moorland.*

Frog Combe

Black Hill

Robin Upright's Hill

Frog Hill

11 *Rejoin the main track back to the car park.*

A

358

Wilmot's Pool

P

4 *Cross over and keep on the track, gently ascending to Higher Hare Knap.*

P

P

3 *Turn right and follow the track downhill.*

2 *Deviate left uphill by Wilmot's Pool to the highest point at 1178 feet (358 m).*

1 *From the car park, bear round to the left on a level broad track.*

61

DULVERTON AND COURT DOWN

4 miles (6½ km) Moderate

Surprisingly few walks actually begin in Dulverton, and the river bank remains frustratingly out of reach for a good ½ mile (800 m) in either direction. The track which forms the first part of this walk continues up the Barle valley to Withypool, but this is a long walk with little alternative but to return the same way.

This walk does, however, include an element of river bank, woodland, ruined buildings, moorland heights, and Dulverton itself. Dulverton has often been named 'The Gateway to Exmoor', and today it is the headquarters of the Exmoor National Park Authority.

Here, there is an information centre and permanent display of all aspects of Exmoor. Beyond, there is a large car park with pedestrian access to the town.

Dulverton is well laid-out with a broad main street, prominent town hall, and the parish church at the top end, terminating the thoroughfare. This was rebuilt in 1855 apart from the tower.

Two famous inns gave rise to the saying that at Dulverton the 'Lion' lies down with the 'Lamb' but this no longer holds good; the 'Lamb' has closed its doors and has been converted to flats.

It is an interesting small town to explore with several narrow alleyways and a good mix of shops. It is also the home of the Exmoor Society which keeps a watchful eye on all developments concerning Exmoor from its offices in the Parish Rooms.

A The track leading steeply uphill is an old pack-horse route leading from Dulverton to Anstey's Common. When the Devon wool industry was at its height in the seventeenth century, wool was transported around the West Country by means of strings of horses heavily laden with panniers piled high with fleeces.

B Kennel Farm formed part of the Northmoor Estate and housed the pack of foxhounds belonging to the estate. North-moor was once owned by Sir Frederick Wills of the Bristol tobacco family and, when his son became a peer, he took the title of Lord Dulverton.

C There are two bridges at this junction, both equally attractive. The road is carried across the Barle on an iron bridge, unusual in this part of England. Adjacent is an ancient pack-horse bridge across a small tributary.

D Court Down is 1036 feet (315 m), its summit marked by a concrete trig column. From here, there are extensive views to the south and west, though northwards is somewhat limited by the hedge. Sometimes Dartmoor is visible across lowland Devon.

E The substantial ruin is Northcombe House, part of the Hollam Estate. Believed to date from the early 1800s, the house was destroyed by fire in the mid-1980s.

Over

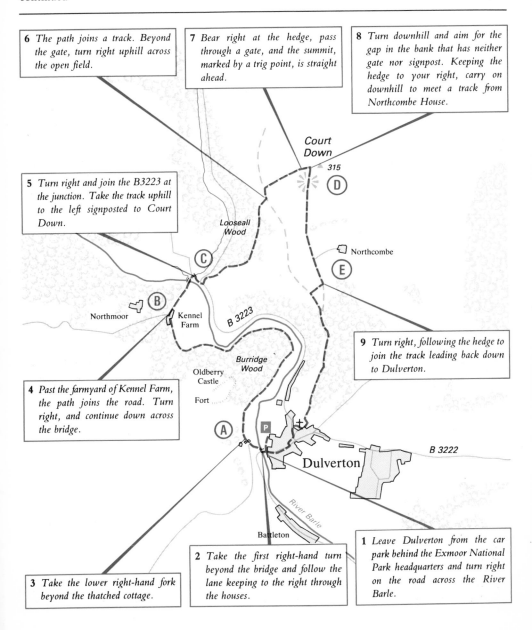

6 *The path joins a track. Beyond the gate, turn right uphill across the open field.*

7 *Bear right at the hedge, pass through a gate, and the summit, marked by a trig point, is straight ahead.*

8 *Turn downhill and aim for the gap in the bank that has neither gate nor signpost. Keeping the hedge to your right, carry on downhill to meet a track from Northcombe House.*

5 *Turn right and join the B3223 at the junction. Take the track uphill to the left signposted to Court Down.*

9 *Turn right, following the hedge to join the track leading back down to Dulverton.*

4 *Past the farmyard of Kennel Farm, the path joins the road. Turn right, and continue down across the bridge.*

1 *Leave Dulverton from the car park behind the Exmoor National Park headquarters and turn right on the road across the River Barle.*

2 *Take the first right-hand turn beyond the bridge and follow the lane keeping to the right through the houses.*

3 *Take the lower right-hand fork beyond the thatched cottage.*

Court Down

315

Northcombe

Looseall Wood

Northmoor

Kennel Farm

B 3223

Burridge Wood

Oldberry Castle

Fort

Dulverton

B 3222

River Barle

Battleton

QUANTOCKS:
LYDEARD HILL
1½ miles (2½ km) Easy

For the very minimum of effort, or even with no effort at all, one of the best views in all Somerset can be experienced. Lydeard Hill, the second highest point of the Quantocks, is reached via the village of West Bagborough by following the road up and turning left at the crossroads, signposted to the car park. Here, at 1100 feet (335 m), the views are very good; by leaving the car and strolling for ten minutes uphill, they become magnificent. The rewards are far greater than is merited by the effort.

West Bagborough is an attractive village with the Rising Sun Inn, plenty of pretty cottages, and a fine church, dating from the fifteenth century with good twentieth-century additions.

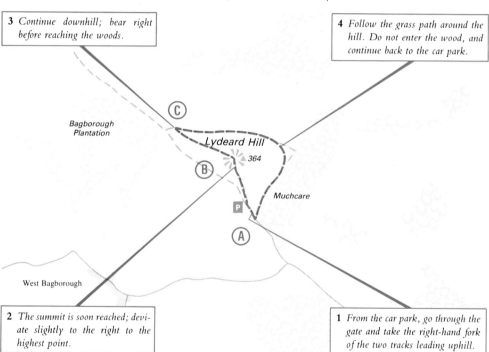

3 Continue downhill; bear right before reaching the woods.

4 Follow the grass path around the hill. Do not enter the wood, and continue back to the car park.

Bagborough Plantation

C

Lydeard Hill
▲ 364

B

Muchcare

P

A

West Bagborough

2 The summit is soon reached; deviate slightly to the right to the highest point.

1 From the car park, go through the gate and take the right-hand fork of the two tracks leading uphill.

A The car park is sited high up on the south-eastern edge of the Quantocks and, even without leaving the car, there are magnificent views. A large information board describes Lydeard Hill and the neighbouring heights.

B The summit, at 1197 feet (364 m), is the second highest point on the Quantocks. To the north-west the view is blocked by Will's Neck but, in all other directions, it is extensive. The beautiful vale, separating the Quantocks from the Brendon Hills, lies below, with the Vale of Taunton and the flat lands of the Somerset levels to the south and north-east.

C The walk can easily be extended to Will's Neck by continuing on the track.

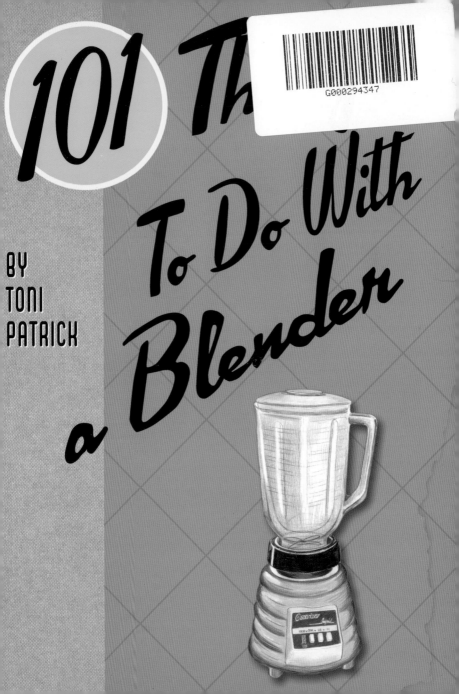

101 Things

To Do With a Blender

BY
TONI
PATRICK

a Blender

101 Things
To Do With
a Blender

101 Things® To Do With a Blender

BY
TONI PATRICK

GIBBS SMITH
TO ENRICH AND INSPIRE HUMANKIND
Salt Lake City │ Charleston │ Santa Fe │ Santa Barbara

First Edition
14 13 12 11 10   20 19 18 17 16 15 14 13 12 11 10 9 8 7 6 5 4 3 2 1

Text © 2010 Toni Patrick
Front cover illustration © 2010 Christine Berrie

Published by
Gibbs Smith
P.O. Box 667
Layton, Utah 84041

1.800.835.4993 orders
www.gibbs-smith.com

Printed and bound in Korea
Gibbs Smith books are printed on either recycled, 100% post-
consumer waste, FSC-certified papers or on paper produced from
a 100% certified sustainable forest/controlled wood source.

Library of Congress Cataloging-in-Publication Data

Patrick, Toni.
  101 things to do with a blender / Toni Patrick. — 1st ed.
    p. cm.
  ISBN-13: 978-1-4236-0690-1
  ISBN-10: 1-4236-0690-6
  1. Blenders (Cookery) I. Title. II. Title: One hundred one things to do
with a blender. III. Title: One hundred and one things to do with a blender.
  TX840.B5P38 2010
  641.5'893—dc22
                        2009034982

As always, I'm sending out big thanks
to my friends and family for your love
and support. I couldn't do what I do
without you doing what you do!

Most especially I would like to thank my
daughter, Robbi, for her enthusiasm and
understanding as we blended and blended
day after day. It was a lot to ask of an infant!

All my love,

Toni

CONTENTS

Dressings

Ranch Dressing 66 • Creamy Italian Dressing 67 • Ginger Dressing 68 • Creamy Cilantro Dressing 69 • Sweet Mustard Dressing 70 • Caesar Dressing 71 • French Dressing 72 • Balsamic Vinaigrette 73 • Peach Poppyseed Dressing 74 • Catalina Dressing 75 • Blue Cheese Dressing 76 • Raspberry Vinaigrette 77

Sauces

Hollandaise Sauce 80 • Apricot Barbecue Sauce 81 • Roasted Red Pepper Sauce 82 • Marinara Sauce 83 • Cranberry Sauce 84 • Applesauce 85 • Creamy Green Chile Sauce 86 • Pesto 87 • Peanut Sauce 88 • Sweet and Sour Sauce 89

Desserts

Moist Cupcakes 92 • Chocolate Cinnamon Cake 93 • Chocolate Date Nut Cake 94 • Cheesecake 95 • Berry Mousse 96 • Chocolate Mousse 97 • Crustless Coconut Pie 98 • Baked Custard 99 • Lemon Pie 100 • Pecan Pie 101 • Pumpkin Pie 102 • Fruity Ice Cream 103 • Strawberry Ice Cream 104 • Mini Nut Cakes 105 • Flan 106 • Chocolate Chip Cookies 107

Drinks

Frozen Lemonade 110 • Strawberry Milk 111 • Grape Froth 112 • Root Beer Smoothie 113 • Piña Colada 114 • Iced Mocha 115 • Pear-Pineapple Smoothie 116 • Frozen Lemon Tea 117 • Strawberry-Banana Smoothie 118 • Chocolate Malt 119 • Orange Julius 120 • Chocolate Shake 121 • Strawberry Cocoa-licious 122 • Hot Chocolate 123 • Spicy Tomato Blend 124 • All-Natural Energy Drink 125

HELPFUL HINTS

1. Remove the base from the regular blender container. Place ingredients in a pint-size mason jar in reverse order. Screw the base onto the mason jar. Make sure it is nice and tight. Invert the jar and place on the blender. Blend as directed. This is especially convenient with sauces, dressings, and dips because you just blend and store!

2. Be sure to add ingredients as listed. Adding liquid ingredients first, followed by fine or powdered ingredients, then finishing with larger ingredients like quartered vegetables helps the mixture blend easier.

3. You may need to pulse a mixture a few times to get the ingredients to begin blending smoothly.

4. Blenders are quick and easy to clean. Just rinse the blender pitcher and add a small amount of dish soap with about 2 cups warm water. Run on high for 30 seconds and rinse.

5. Always leave room in the pitcher for the mixture to expand.

6. Cooked vegetables blend more smoothly than raw vegetables. For a finer soup, sauté vegetables prior to blending or blend after the soup has simmered.

7. Be very careful when blending hot mixtures. Fill the pitcher only half full to avoid spilling over.

8. To reduce fat and calories, substitute reduced-fat foods such as skim milk, light or fat-free sour cream, and light or fat-free cream cheese.

9. When using fresh garlic, I clove garlic equals I teaspoon minced garlic. Using fresh is much more cost effective than using bottled minced garlic.

10. It is possible to roast garlic in the microwave! Peel off paper layers and wrap each whole head in plastic wrap. Cook on high for 1 minute. Let cool and extract pulp by squeezing each clove.

11. For onions, 1/4 cup fresh minced onion equals 2 tablespoons dried minced onion.

12. When measuring herbs, 1/4 cup fresh herbs equals 1 tablespoon dried herbs.

13. Fresh or frozen vegetables, steamed, can be substituted for canned vegetables.

14. As always, be creative! Most ingredients can be adjusted to your own liking.

BREAKFAST

BUTTERMILK PANCAKES

I	**egg**
I cup	**buttermilk**
$^{1}/_{2}$ teaspoon	**salt**
I teaspoon	**baking soda**
I teaspoon	**sugar**
I teaspoon	**vanilla**
I tablespoon	**vegetable oil**
I cup	**flour**

In a blender, add egg and blend on high until well blended. As blender is running, add buttermilk, salt, baking soda, sugar, vanilla, and oil. Once thoroughly blended, turn off blender. Add flour and pulse lightly until flour is mixed in. Do not over blend. Pour $^{1}/_{4}$ cup batter into a skillet over medium heat. Once most of the bubbles pop, flip pancake and cook about I minute on the other side. Makes 4 servings.

SUNRISE BOOSTER

1	**small banana**
1/2 cup	**fresh or frozen strawberries**
1/2 cup	**milk**
1/4 cup	**sweetened corn flake cereal**
1/4 teaspoon	**vanilla extract**
2	**ice cubes**

Place all ingredients, in the order listed above, into a blender. Cover and blend on high until mixture is smooth. Serve immediately. Makes 2 servings.

CORNMEAL WAFFLES

1	**egg**
3/4 cup	**milk**
1/4 cup	**vegetable oil**
1 cup	**flour**
2 tablespoons	**cornmeal**
2 teaspoons	**baking powder**
2 teaspoons	**sugar**
1/4 teaspoon	**salt**

Preheat a waffle iron. Put all ingredients into a blender. Cover and process at a medium-high speed until dry ingredients are moistened. Do not over blend. Pour 1/2 cup batter into waffle iron and then close; bake until golden and serve with syrup or honey. Makes 4 servings.

CRUSTLESS QUICHE

I cup	**grated cheddar cheese**
6 pieces	**bacon,** cooked and crumbled
I 1/2 cups	**milk**
4	**eggs**
1/2 cup	**flour**
1/2 cup	**chopped onion**
2 tablespoons	**butter or margarine**
1/2 teaspoon	**salt**
1/8 teaspoon	**pepper**

Preheat oven to 350 degrees.

Sprinkle cheese and bacon over the bottom of a well-buttered 9-inch pie plate. Combine milk, eggs, flour, onion, butter, salt, and pepper in a blender. Cover and blend until mixture is smooth, stopping and scraping sides as necessary. Pour over cheese and bacon in pie plate. Bake for 30–35 minutes. Makes 6 servings.

CREPES

1 cup	**cold water**
1/2 teaspoon	**salt**
1 cup	**cold milk**
2 cups	**flour**
4 large	**eggs**
4 tablespoons	**melted butter**
2 cups	**frozen sweetened strawberries,** thawed and sliced
	whipped topping
	powdered sugar

Place all ingredients except strawberries, whipped topping, and powdered sugar in a blender and blend until smooth. Refrigerate for 2 hours before cooking. Pour approximately 3 tablespoons batter into a hot, lightly buttered or oiled 7-inch pan. Tilt and swirl pan until batter covers the bottom in a thin film. Cook until lightly browned; turn and cook 30 seconds. Place 1/4 cup strawberries in center of crepe and roll. Serve with whipped topping or a sprinkle of powdered sugar. Makes 4–6 servings.

MIGAS

2 bunches	**green onions,** sliced
3 tablespoons	**butter or margarine**
12	**eggs**
1 tablespoon	**cumin**
1 tablespoon	**garlic powder**
1 tablespoon	**dried sweet basil**
2 cups	**grated cheddar cheese**
2½ cups	**slightly crumbled tortilla chips**
1½ cups	**picante sauce**

In a frying pan, saute the onions in butter until tender. In a blender, mix together the eggs, cumin, garlic, basil, and onions. Pour egg mixture into a frying pan over medium heat and stir to scramble. Add cheese, tortilla chips, and picante sauce. Continuously scrape pan with spatula until the eggs are fluffy. Serve immediately. Makes 8 servings.

BAKED FRENCH TOAST

4	**eggs**
1 1/2 cups	**milk**
1/2 cup	**heavy cream**
3 teaspoons	**cinnamon**
3 teaspoons	**vanilla**
8 pieces	**Texas toast,** each cut into 9 pieces

In a blender, mix together all ingredients except bread until fluffy. In a greased 9 x 13-inch glass baking dish, evenly distribute bread pieces. Pour egg mixture over bread, making sure to soak each piece. Refrigerate at least 1 hour, or overnight.

Preheat oven to 350 degrees.

Bake for 45 minutes, or until a toothpick inserted in the center comes out clean. Makes 4 servings.

CREAMY SCRAMBLED EGGS

6	**eggs**
1/2	**medium yellow onion**
1/4 cup	**butter or margarine**
1 package (3 ounces)	**cream cheese,** softened
1/4 cup	**milk**
1/4 teaspoon	**salt**
1/8 teaspoon	**pepper**

Mix together all ingredients in a blender until thoroughly blended. Pour mixture into a large frying pan over medium heat and stir to scramble. Continuously scrape pan with spatula until the eggs are fluffy. Serve immediately. Makes 4 servings.

GERMAN PANCAKES

2 large	**eggs**
3/4 cup	**milk**
4 tablespoons	**flour**
2 tablespoons	**sugar**
dash	**salt**
	powdered sugar

Place all ingredients except powdered sugar in a blender and pulse until smooth. Let batter rest about 5 minutes before using so it is not too frothy. Spray a large frying pan with cooking spray. Place 1/4 cup batter in skillet, tilting to evenly distribute. Once it is light brown, flip pancake and cook other side until light brown. Sprinkle with powdered sugar and serve. Makes 4 servings.

BANANA NUT BREAD

2 ½ cups	**sifted self-rising flour**
3 teaspoons	**baking powder**
½ teaspoon	**salt**
I cup	**chopped walnuts**
I cup	**sugar**
⅓ cup	**butter or margarine,** softened
I	**egg**
½ cup	**milk**
3	**bananas**

Preheat oven to 350 degrees.

In a bowl, mix together the flour, baking powder, and salt; set aside. Place nuts in a blender and pulse until chopped. Add nuts to the dry ingredients. Put the sugar, butter, egg, milk, and bananas into blender. Cover and blend until mixture is smooth, stopping and scraping sides as necessary. Add flour mixture and pulse until lightly mixed. Pour batter into a greased 9 x 5-inch loaf pan. Bake for I hour, or until a toothpick inserted in the center comes out clean. Makes I loaf.

ZUCCHINI BREAD

3	**eggs**
I cup	**oil**
2 teaspoons	**baking soda**
I teaspoon	**salt**
$^1/_4$ teaspoon	**baking powder**
3 teaspoons	**cinnamon**
I $^1/_2$ cups	**sugar**
I small	**zucchini**
2 teaspoons	**vanilla**
I cup	**walnuts,** optional
2 cups	**self-rising flour**

Preheat oven to 350 degrees.

Place all ingredients except the flour in a blender. Cover and blend until mixture is smooth, stopping and scraping sides as necessary. Pour into bowl, add flour. Stir until smooth. Bake in a greased 9 x 5-inch loaf pan for 60–70 minutes, or until a toothpick inserted in the center comes out clean. Makes I loaf.

APPLESAUCE MUFFINS

I	**egg**
3/4 cup	**milk**
I cup	**sugar**
I 1/2 teaspoons	**cinnamon**
1/2 cup	**applesauce**
I 1/2 cups	**self-rising flour**

Preheat oven to 350 degrees.

Put all ingredients into a blender. Cover and blend until mixture is smooth, stopping and scraping sides as necessary. Pour batter into lined muffin tins and bake until golden brown, about 20–25 minutes. Makes I2 muffins.

DIPS & SPREADS

FRENCH ONION DIP

2 tablespoons	**half-and-half**
2 teaspoons	**Worcestershire sauce**
1 1/4 cups	**sour cream**
1/4 cup	**mayonnaise**
dash	**cayenne pepper**
1 teaspoon	**minced garlic**
1 cup	**French fried onions**

Place ingredients, in the order listed above, into a blender. Cover and blend on high until mixture is smooth. Transfer mixture to a serving dish and chill for 1 hour. Serve with cut-up veggies or potato chips. Makes 2 1/2 cups.

BEAN DIP

1 can (10.5 ounces)	**diced tomatoes,** drained
1/2 cup	**sour cream**
1 can (10.5 ounces)	**refried beans**
1/8 teaspoon	**Tabasco**
2 cups	**grated cheddar cheese**

Place ingredients except cheese, in the order listed above, into a blender. Cover and blend until mixture is smooth, stopping and scraping sides as necessary. Place in a slow cooker on low heat and add cheese; stir together. Serve hot with tortilla chips. Makes 3 cups.

VEGETABLE DIP

I cup	**mayonnaise**
I cup	**sour cream**
3 tablespoons	**lemon juice**
$1/2$ teaspoon	**garlic powder**
$1/2$ teaspoon	**dried dill weed**
I teaspoon	**Italian dressing mix**

Place ingredients, in the order listed above, into a blender. Cover and blend on high until mixture is smooth. Transfer mixture to a serving dish and chill for I hour. Serve with cut-up veggies or crackers. Makes 2 cups.

CREAMY SHRIMP DIP

I package (3 ounces)	**cream cheese,** softened
2 tablespoons	**mayonnaise**
I tablespoon	**ketchup**
I teaspoon	**mustard**
dash	**garlic powder**
I cup	**chopped canned shrimp**
$^1/_4$ cup	**chopped celery**
I teaspoon	**chopped onion**

Place ingredients, in the order listed above, into a blender. Cover and blend on high until mixture is smooth. Transfer mixture to a serving dish and chill for I hour. Serve with chips or crackers. Makes 2 cups.

GUACAMOLE

3 teaspoons	**minced garlic**
3	**green onions**
$^1/_2$	**jalapeño pepper,** seeded
1	**avocado,** peeled and pitted
2 tablespoons	**lemon juice**
$^1/_4$ teaspoon	**chili powder**
$^1/_2$ teaspoon	**salt**
1	**tomato,** quartered

Place ingredients, in the order listed above, into a blender. Cover and blend on high until mixture is smooth. Transfer mixture to a serving dish and serve with tortilla chips or as a side for tacos and burritos. Makes 1$^1/_2$–2 cups.

ARTICHOKE DIP

¹/₂ cup	**mayonnaise**
¹/₂ cup	**sour cream**
I envelope	**Italian dressing mix**
I can (16 ounces)	**artichoke hearts,** drained
¹/₂ cup	**grated Parmesan cheese**

Place ingredients, in the order listed above, into a blender. Cover and blend on high until mixture is smooth. Transfer mixture to a serving dish and chill for I hour. Serve with veggies, crackers, or thinly sliced toasted bread. Makes I¹/₂ cups.

HUMMUS

1 can (15.5 ounces)	**garbanzo beans,** drained and liquid reserved
1 package (3 ounces)	**cream cheese,** softened
1 tablespoon	**lemon juice**
$1/4$ cup	**chopped green onions**
2 teaspoons	**prepared horseradish**
$1/2$ teaspoon	**salt**

Place ingredients, in the order listed above, into a blender. Cover and blend on high until mixture is smooth. Transfer mixture to a serving dish and chill for 1 hour. Serve with pita wedges, chips, crackers, or spread onto sandwiches. Makes 2 cups.

SALSA

1/2	**onion,** quartered
1/2 cup	**chopped fresh cilantro**
2 cans (10 ounces each)	**diced tomatoes,** drained
1 teaspoon	**minced garlic**
1/2 teaspoon	**lime juice**

Place ingredients, in the order listed above, into a blender. Cover and blend on high until mixture is smooth. Transfer mixture to a serving dish and serve with chips or as a side to tacos and burritos, or nachos. Makes 1 1/2 cups.

WARM GARLIC SPREAD

4	**whole heads garlic**
I cup	**evaporated fat-free milk**
1/2 teaspoon	**salt**
1/8 teaspoon	**black pepper**
2	**large egg yolks**
I	**large egg**

Preheat oven to 350 degrees.

Remove white papery skin from garlic heads (do not peel or separate the cloves). Wrap each head separately in foil. Bake for I hour; cool I0 minutes. Separate cloves and then squeeze to extract garlic; discard skins.

Combine all ingredients in a blender and blend until smooth. Pour garlic mixture into a shallow I 1/2-quart baking dish coated with cooking spray. Place dish in a large baking pan and pour hot water into pan around baking dish to a depth of I inch. Bake for 30 minutes, or just until set in the center. Remove from pan and then cool briefly on a wire rack. Spread on French bread and serve warm. Makes 8 servings.

ALMOND FETA CHEESE SPREAD

I cup	**whole blanched almonds**
$1/4$ cup	**lemon juice**
3 tablespoons	**olive oil**
I teaspoon	**minced garlic**
I $1/4$ teaspoons	**salt**
$1/2$ cup	**water**
8 ounces	**feta cheese**

Preheat oven to 350 degrees.

Place almonds in a bowl and cover with 3 inches of water; let soak 24 hours and then drain and rinse. Puree almonds with remaining ingredients in a blender for 3–6 minutes, or until really creamy. Place a triple layer of cheesecloth in a strainer and spoon mixture onto cheesecloth. Bring sides together, twist into an orange-size ball, and secure with a twist tie; place in a bowl for draining. Chill for 12 hours. Line baking sheet with parchment and transfer almond ball from cheesecloth. Place in an 8 x 8-inch glass baking dish and bake 40 minutes, or until top is slightly firm. Cool and then chill in refrigerator. Serve with crackers or toasted bread. Makes 2 cups.

FRUIT DIP

$1/4$ cup	**whipping cream**
$3/4$ cup	**cottage cheese**
$1/2$ cup	**sour cream**
$1 1/2$ tablespoons	**sugar**

Place ingredients, in the order listed above, into a blender. Cover and blend on high until mixture is smooth. Transfer mixture to a serving dish and chill for 1 hour. Serve with fruit for dipping. Makes $1 1/2$ cups.

SOUPS

CAULIFLOWER SOUP

4 cups	**chicken or vegetable broth**
1 teaspoon	**minced garlic**
1/2 cup	**heavy cream**
1	**medium red onion,** quartered
1	**small head cauliflower,** steamed and chopped
	salt and black pepper, to taste

Place ingredients, using 1/2 the head of cauliflower, in the order listed above, into a blender. Cover and blend on high until mixture is smooth. Transfer mixture to a large pot, add remaining cauliflower, and bring to a boil over high heat. Reduce heat to medium and simmer for 30–45 minutes. Makes 6 servings.

CREAM OF BROCCOLI SOUP

1 1/3 cups	**chicken broth**
1 teaspoon	**salt**
1/4 teaspoon	**finely crumbled dried basil**
1/8 teaspoon	**black pepper**
1 package (10 ounces)	**frozen chopped broccoli,** thawed
1/2 cup	**chopped onion**
2 tablespoons	**butter or margarine**
2 tablespoons	**flour**
1/2 cup	**half-and-half**
1/2 cup	**grated cheddar cheese**

Place the first 6 ingredients, in the order listed above, into a blender. Cover and blend on high until mixture is smooth.

In a large pot, melt the butter. Add flour and stir until it just begins to brown. Transfer blended mixture to the pot and bring to a boil over high heat. Reduce heat to medium and simmer for 30–45 minutes. Add half-and-half and cheese. Return to a simmer, stirring constantly, until cheese is completely melted. Serve immediately. Makes 4 servings.

GRANDMA'S BEEFY VEGETABLE SOUP

I can (10.5 ounces)	**beef broth**
I can (14.5 ounces)	**diced tomatoes,** drained
I	**small onion,** quartered
2	**carrots**
2 stalks	**celery**
I	**green pepper,** quartered and seeded

Place ingredients, in the order listed above, into a blender. Cover and blend on high until mixture is smooth. Transfer mixture to a large pot and bring to a boil over high heat. Reduce heat to medium and simmer for 30–45 minutes. Makes 6 servings.

VARIATION: For a chunky version, add cut-up leftover roast and a can of diced potatoes, drained.

TOMATO SOUP

1 can (14.5 ounces)	**diced tomatoes,** undrained
1½ cups	**water**
½ cup	**chopped onion**
1 teaspoon	**minced garlic**
⅛ teaspoon	**white pepper**
⅛ teaspoon	**salt**
dash	**Tabasco**

Place ingredients, in the order listed above, into a blender. Cover and blend on high until mixture is smooth. Transfer mixture to a large pot and bring to a boil over high heat. Reduce heat to medium and simmer for 15–20 minutes. Makes 4 servings.

PEA SOUP

I can (17 ounces)	**green peas,** undrained
1 1/2 cups	**milk**
2 tablespoons	**butter or margarine**
2 teaspoons	**flour**
1/2 teaspoon	**salt**
1/2 teaspoon	**nutmeg**
1/4 teaspoon	**sugar**
I	**small onion,** peeled and quartered

Place ingredients, in the order listed above, into a blender. Cover and blend on high until mixture is smooth. Transfer mixture to a large pot and bring to a boil over high heat. Reduce heat to medium and simmer for 30–45 minutes. Makes 4 servings.

RED PEPPER SOUP

2 teaspoons	**olive oil**
1 1/2 cups	**chopped onions**
1/4 cup	**finely chopped shallots**
1 teaspoon	**minced garlic**
1 can (14 ounces)	**chicken broth**
1 can (14 ounces)	**beef broth**
1 tablespoon	**tomato paste**
1/2 cup	**chopped celery**
1/2 cup	**sliced carrot**
1 jar (16 ounces)	**roasted red peppers**
1 teaspoon	**Italian seasoning**
1/2 teaspoon	**salt**
1/4 teaspoon	**freshly ground black pepper**
1/4 teaspoon	**Tabasco or your favorite hot sauce**

Heat oil in a large saucepan over medium heat. Add onions, shallots, and garlic; cook 3 minutes, stirring occasionally. Place remaining ingredients, in the order listed above, into a blender. Add sautéed mixture, cover, and blend on high until mixture is smooth. Transfer mixture to a large pot and bring to a boil over high heat. Reduce heat to medium and simmer for 30–45 minutes. Makes 6 servings.

POTATO SOUP

6	**medium white potatoes,** peeled and cubed
2 cups	**water**
2½ cups	**chicken broth**
3 stalks	**celery**
1	**large white onion,** quartered
4 tablespoons	**butter or margarine**
1 tablespoon	**dried dill**
1½ teaspoons	**salt**
1½ teaspoons	**white pepper**
1 teaspoon	**garlic salt**
2 cups	**half-and-half**
2 cups	**grated sharp cheddar cheese**
6 strips	**bacon,** cooked and crumbled

Place potatoes in a large soup pot and add enough water to cover completely. Bring to a boil and cook for 7 minutes; drain. Place half of the potatoes and remaining ingredients, in the order listed above, into a blender. Cover and blend until mixture is smooth, stopping and scraping sides as necessary. Transfer mixture into the pot with the remaining potatoes and bring to a boil over medium-high heat. Reduce heat to medium and simmer for 30–45 minutes, stirring regularly. Makes 6 servings.

GAZPACHO

1/2	**green bell pepper,** quartered and seeded
3	**tomatoes,** quartered
1	**cucumber,** chunked
1/2 cup	**cold vegetable stock**
3 tablespoons	**rice vinegar**
1/2 teaspoon	**chili powder**
2 tablespoons	**vegetable oil**
1/4 teaspoon	**salt**

Place ingredients, in the order listed above, into a blender. Cover and blend on high until mixture reaches the desired consistency. Transfer mixture to a bowl and chill for at least 2 hours. Makes 4 servings.

CREAM OF CHICKEN SOUP

¹/₄ cup	**chopped onion**
¹/₄ cup	**chopped celery**
I teaspoon	**minced garlic**
6 tablespoons	**butter or margarine**
¹/₃ cup	**flour**
I cup	**cooked and chopped chicken**
¹/₄ teaspoon	**white pepper**
¹/₄ teaspoon	**black pepper**
¹/₂ teaspoon	**salt**
¹/₈ teaspoon	**ground cayenne pepper**
I cup	**half-and-half**
3 cups	**chicken broth**

Place the onion, celery, and garlic into a blender and puree. Melt butter in a large saucepan over medium heat. Transfer onion mixture to pan with butter and sauté until soft, about 2 minutes. Add flour, mix well, and cook for 3 minutes more, stirring regularly. Return to blender and add chicken, remaining seasonings, half-and-half, and broth, blending until creamy. Pour mixture back into saucepan and cook over medium heat, stirring regularly, until it thickens and comes to a boil. Reduce heat to low and simmer until ready to serve. Makes 4 servings.

VARIATION: For a chunky version, do not blend the chicken.

CREAM OF MUSHROOM SOUP

¹/₄ cup	**butter or margarine**
¹/₄	**onion,** chopped
I can (12 ounces)	**evaporated milk**
2 cans (8 ounces each)	**mushroom stems and pieces,** with liquid
¹/₄ cup	**flour**
I teaspoon	**seasoning salt**
I teaspoon	**parsley**
¹/₂ teaspoon	**white pepper**

Melt butter in large saucepan over medium heat. Add onion and cook for 1−2 minutes or until tender; remove from heat. Transfer mixture to a blender, add remaining ingredients, and blend. Return to saucepan and cook over medium heat, stirring constantly, until mixture comes to a boil. Serve when mixture thickens. Makes 4 servings

QUICK CHILI

1 pound	**hamburger**
1 can (14.5 ounces)	**diced tomatoes,** drained
1	**large onion,** quartered
1 large	**green bell pepper,** quartered and seeded
1 can (14 ounces)	**red kidney beans**
2 tablespoons	**chili powder**
1/8 teaspoon	**garlic powder**
1 teaspoon	**mustard**

Brown the hamburger, drain, and set aside. Place half of the beans and remaining ingredients except hamburger, in the order listed above, into a blender. Cover and blend on high until mixture is smooth. Transfer mixture to a large pot, add hamburger and remaining beans, and bring to a boil over high heat. Reduce heat to medium and simmer for 30–45 minutes. Makes 4 servings.

PURELY VEGGIE VEGETABLE SOUP

I cube	**vegetable bouillon**
I ½ cups	**hot water**
I teaspoon	**olive oil**
	juice from ½ lemon
I stalk	**celery**
I	**large carrot**
½	**red bell pepper,** seeded
½	**medium yellow squash**

Place ingredients, in the order listed above, into a blender. Cover and blend on high until mixture is smooth. Transfer mixture to a large pot and bring to a boil over high heat. Reduce heat to medium and simmer for 30–45 minutes. Makes 2 servings.

ENTREES
& SIDES

GREEN PEPPER MEATBALLS

I	**green bell pepper,** seeded
I	**onion**
I	**egg**
I pound	**ground beef**
2 cups	**marinara sauce**
I cup	**water**

Preheat oven to 350 degrees.

Place bell pepper, onion, and egg into a blender. Cover and blend on high until mixture is smooth.

In a large bowl, mix together the meat and blender mixture. Form into 24 meatballs. Arrange in a single layer on a shallow baking sheet. Pour marinara sauce and water over top. Cover with foil. Bake for I hour. Makes 4–6 servings.

BARBECUE BEEF

1 bottle (12 ounces)	**chili sauce**
1 can (8 ounces)	**tomato sauce**
1/8 cup	**sliced onion**
1/2	**green bell pepper,** seeded
1 tablespoon	**Worcestershire sauce**
1/8 teaspoon	**dry mustard**
2 tablespoons	**grape jelly**
1/4 teaspoon	**salt**
2 cups	**cooked and cubed roast beef**
8	**hamburger buns**

Combine all ingredients except buns in blender. Blend until beef is just chopped.

In a saucepan, simmer mixture over medium heat for 15–20 minutes. Spoon onto buns and serve. Makes 8 servings.

CHEESEBURGER BAKE

2 pounds	**ground beef**
I can (15 ounces)	**tomato sauce**
¹/₂	**small onion,** cut in half
I teaspoon	**salt**
I teaspoon	**sugar**
¹/₈ teaspoon	**garlic salt**
I cup	**instant rice,** uncooked
¹/₃ cup	**milk**
I cup	**cottage cheese**
I package (3 ounces)	**cream cheese,** cubed
¹/₂	**green bell pepper,** seeded
¹/₂ cup	**grated sharp cheddar cheese**

Preheat oven to 350 degrees.

Brown beef in a large skillet; drain. Place tomato sauce, onion, salt, sugar, and garlic salt in a blender and blend until onion is just chopped. Add to beef along with the instant rice. Mix and place half the mixture in an 8 x 8-inch baking dish. Place milk, cottage cheese and cream cheese in blender and blend until smooth. Add bell pepper and blend until pepper is chopped. Pour mixture over beef in pan. Top with remaining beef and sprinkle with cheese. Bake for 35 minutes. Makes 4–6 servings.

HAM ROLLS

8	**large sourdough rolls**
$1/2$ cup	**mayonnaise**
$1/2$ teaspoon	**mild chili powder**
1	**hard-boiled egg,** shelled
2	**green onions**
8 slices	**American cheese**
$1\frac{1}{2}$ cups	**cooked and diced ham,** divided

Preheat oven to 400 degrees.

Slice top off of rolls and scoop out centers; set aside.

In a blender, combine the mayonnaise, chili powder, egg, onions, and cheese; blend until creamy. Add roll centers and blend until mixed. Add $1/2$ cup ham and mix until ham is chopped. Repeat with rest of ham. Spoon into rolls and wrap in foil. Bake for 20–25 minutes. Makes 8 servings.

VEGETABLE FRITTERS

	vegetable oil, for frying
1 cup	**milk**
1	**egg**
2 cups	**flour**
2 teaspoons	**baking powder**
3/4 teaspoon	**salt**
1/2 cup	**lightly chopped broccoli**
1/2 cup	**lightly chopped cauliflower**
1/2 cup	**grated cheddar cheese**

In a large frying pan or deep fryer, heat oil to 375 degrees.

Place remaining ingredients in a blender and blend until mixture is uniform. Using a tablespoon, drop mixture into oil. Cook until golden brown, about 3 minutes, flipping to brown evenly. Makes about 24 fritters.

POPOVER ROLLS

I cup	**milk**
3	**eggs**
I tablespoon	**vegetable oil**
$^1/_2$ teaspoon	**salt**
$^1/_8$ teaspoon	**sugar**
I cup	**flour**

Preheat oven to 400 degrees.

Place all ingredients except flour in a blender. Blend until well mixed. Add flour and pulse until smooth. Do not over blend. Pour batter into muffin tins, filling each about half full. Bake for 25–30 minutes. Makes 6 rolls.

POTATO CASSEROLE

1 cup	**milk**
3	**eggs**
1 1/2 teaspoons	**salt**
1/8 teaspoon	**pepper**
1 cup	**cubed cheddar cheese**
2 tablespoons	**butter or margarine,** softened
1/2	**green bell pepper,** quartered and seeded
1	**small onion,** quartered
4	**medium russet potatoes,** peeled and cubed

Preheat oven to 350 degrees.

Place all ingredients, in the order listed above, into a blender. Cover and blend on high until mixture is smooth. Pour into a 9 x 13-inch glass dish and bake for 60 minutes. Makes 6 servings.

STUFFED ZUCCHINI

3	**medium zucchini**
1	**egg**
$^1/_2$ cup	**grated sharp cheddar cheese**
$^1/_8$ cup	**sliced onion**
$^1/_8$ teaspoon	**parsley**
$^1/_2$ teaspoon	**salt**
$^1/_8$ teaspoon	**pepper**
24	**saltine crackers**
1 tablespoon	**butter or margarine,** melted

Preheat oven to 350 degrees.

Cut off zucchini ends and discard; slice zucchini in half lengthwise. Core and set skins aside. Place zucchini cores in a blender with all ingredients except crackers and butter. Blend until zucchini is chopped.

In a bowl, crumble crackers and set $^1/_4$ cup aside. Add zucchini mixture to crackers in bowl and combine. Spoon mixture into zucchini skins. Combine remaining cracker crumbs with butter and sprinkle over zucchini. Bake for about 35 minutes, or until zucchini skins are tender. Makes 6 servings.

COLESLAW

½ cup	**vinegar**
½ cup	**mayonnaise**
2 stalks	**celery**
	salt and pepper, to taste
1	**onion,** quartered
1	**green bell pepper,** quartered and seeded
½ head	**red cabbage,** sliced into thin strips
½ head	**white cabbage,** sliced into thin strips
1	**large carrot,** thinly sliced

Mix the first 6 ingredients in a blender until creamy. Place remaining ingredients in a large bowl and toss with creamy mixture. Serve chilled. Makes 8 servings.

TUNA PASTA SALAD

¹/₂ cup	**mayonnaise**
I can (7 ounces)	**tuna,** drained
I	**pickle spear**
I stalk	**celery**
2 slices	**onion**
2	**hard-boiled eggs,** shelled
¹/₂ cup	**grated cheddar cheese**
I cup	**dry elbow macaroni,** cooked, drained, and cooled

Combine the mayonnaise, tuna, pickle, celery, onion, and eggs in a blender and blend until mixed.

In a bowl, combine tuna mixture with cheese and cooked macaroni. Serve chilled. Makes 2 servings.

CUCUMBER SALAD

4 boxes (3 ounces each)	**lemon gelatin**
5 cups	**boiling water**
1	**large cucumber,** peeled

Place boiling water and gelatin in a blender. Blend until dissolved. Add cucumber and blend until pureed. Transfer mixture to a serving dish or mold and then chill for 2 hours. Garnish with cucumber slices, if desired. Makes 4–6 servings.

FRUIT SALAD

I can (8 ounces)	**pineapple chunks,** with juice
I can (16 ounces)	**apricot halves,** drained
6 ounces	**cream cheese,** softened
I small box	**apricot gelatin**
I small box	**orange gelatin**
I cup	**boiling water**

Place the pineapple, apricots, and cream cheese in a blender and blend until smooth. Dissolve gelatin in boiling water and add to blender. Cover and blend on high until mixture is smooth. Transfer mixture to a serving dish or mold and then chill for 2 hours. Makes 6–8 servings.

DRESSINGS

RANCH DRESSING

1 1/2 cups	**mayonnaise**
1/2 cup	**sour cream**
1/4 cup	**heavy cream**
2 tablespoons	**lemon juice**
1/2 teaspoon	**garlic powder**
1/2 teaspoon	**dried dill weed**

Place ingredients, in the order listed above, into a blender. Cover and blend on high until mixture is smooth. Transfer mixture to a serving dish; chill for 2 hours. Makes 2 cups.

CREAMY ITALIAN DRESSING

I cup	**mayonnaise**
2 tablespoons	**red wine vinegar**
$3/4$ teaspoon	**Italian seasoning**
$1/4$ teaspoon	**garlic powder**
I tablespoon	**granulated sugar**
$1/4$ teaspoon	**salt**
$1/8$ teaspoon	**pepper**
7	**green onions**

Place ingredients, in the order listed above, into a blender. Cover and blend on high until mixture is smooth. Transfer mixture to a serving dish; chill for 2 hours. Makes I $1/2$ cups.

GINGER DRESSING

½ cup	**sesame or soy oil**
¼ cup	**soy sauce**
⅓ cup	**diced onion**
¼ cup	**diced celery**
3 tablespoons	**rice wine vinegar**
½ teaspoon	**ground ginger**
2 teaspoons	**sugar**
⅛ teaspoon	**lemon juice**
½ teaspoon	**ketchup**
¼ teaspoon	**black pepper**

Place ingredients, in the order listed above, into a blender. Cover and blend on high until mixture is smooth. Transfer mixture to a serving dish; chill for 2 hours. Makes 1½ cups.

CREAMY CILANTRO DRESSING

½ cup	**fresh cilantro**
¼ cup	**buttermilk**
¼ cup	**mayonnaise**
⅛ teaspoon	**sugar**
dash	**Tabasco**
	salt and pepper, to taste

Place ingredients, in the order listed above, into a blender. Cover and blend on high until mixture is smooth. Transfer mixture to a serving dish; chill for 2 hours. Makes I cup.

SWEET MUSTARD DRESSING

¹/₄ cup	**extra virgin olive oil**
¹/₂ cup	**salad oil**
2 ¹/₂ tablespoons	**mustard**
3 tablespoons	**maple syrup**
2 tablespoons	**white vinegar**
¹/₄ cup	**half-and-half**
	salt, to taste
I teaspoon	**minced garlic**

Place ingredients, in the order listed above, into a blender. Cover and blend on high until mixture is smooth. Transfer mixture to a serving dish; chill for 2 hours. Makes I cup.

CAESAR DRESSING

3 tablespoons	**mayonnaise**
2 teaspoons	**minced garlic**
4	**anchovy fillets**
$1/2$ cup	**extra virgin olive oil**
$1/8$ teaspoon	**salt**
$1/4$ teaspoon	**pepper**
1	**lemon slice with peel**
$1/4$ cup	**grated Parmesan cheese**

In a blender, mix the mayonnaise, garlic, and anchovies into a paste. Place remaining ingredients, in the order listed above, into the blender. Cover and blend on high until mixture is smooth. Transfer mixture to a serving dish; chill for 2 hours. Makes 1 cup.

FRENCH DRESSING

I cup	**vegetable oil**
3/4 cup	**ketchup**
1/2 cup	**white vinegar**
1/2 cup	**sugar**
1/2 teaspoon	**onion salt**
I tablespoon	**lemon juice**
2 tablespoons	**mustard**
1/2 teaspoon	**garlic powder**
I tablespoon	**chili powder**

Place ingredients, in the order listed above, into a blender. Cover and blend on high until mixture is smooth. Transfer mixture to a serving dish; chill for 2 hours. Makes 3 cups.

BALSAMIC VINAIGRETTE

I cup	**olive oil**
5 teaspoons	**minced garlic**
1/8 cup	**sliced yellow onion**
2 tablespoons	**balsamic vinegar**
2 teaspoons	**black pepper**
I tablespoon	**oregano,** dried
I teaspoon	**parsley,** dried
I tablespoon	**basil,** dried
I tablespoon	**grated Parmesan cheese**
I tablespoon	**red wine vinegar**

Place ingredients, in the order listed above, into a blender. Cover and blend on high until mixture is smooth. Transfer mixture to a serving dish; chill for 2 hours. Makes 2 cups.

PEACH POPPYSEED DRESSING

1	**large peach,** pitted
1/4 cup	**sugar**
1/4 cup	**apple juice**
2 tablespoons	**cider vinegar**
1/8 cup	**sliced sweet onion**
1/2 teaspoon	**dry mustard**
1/4 teaspoon	**salt**
1 tablespoon	**olive oil**
1 tablespoon	**poppy seeds**

Place all ingredients except poppy seeds, in the order listed above, into a blender. Cover and blend on high until mixture is smooth. Add poppy seeds and pulse until mixed. Transfer mixture to a serving dish; chill for 2 hours. Makes 2 cups.

CATALINA DRESSING

1 ⅓ cups	**ketchup**
⅓ cup	**red wine vinegar**
⅓ cup	**honey**
dash	**Worcestershire sauce**
pinch	**ground cloves**
3 tablespoons	**finely grated onion**
	salt, to taste
1 cup	**vegetable oil**

Place all ingredients, in the order listed above, into a blender, adding the oil slowly. Cover and blend on high until mixture is smooth. Transfer mixture to a serving dish; chill for 2 hours. Makes 2 cups.

BLUE CHEESE DRESSING

I cup	**buttermilk**
I cup	**sour cream**
I ½ teaspoons	**minced garlic**
⅛ teaspoon	**sugar**
I tablespoon	**paprika**
I teaspoon	**salt**
3 tablespoons	**blue cheese crumbles**

Place all ingredients except blue cheese, in the order listed above, into a blender. Cover and blend on high until mixture is smooth. Add blue cheese and pulse until mixed. Transfer mixture to a serving dish; chill for 2 hours. Makes 2 cups.

RASPBERRY VINAIGRETTE

¹/₂ cup	**vegetable oil**
6	**raspberries**
3 tablespoons	**raspberry vinegar**
2 tablespoons	**seedless raspberry jam**
1 tablespoon	**sugar**
1 tablespoon	**Dijon mustard**
¹/₄ teaspoon	**onion powder**

Place all ingredients, in the order listed above, into a blender. Cover and blend on high until mixture is smooth. Transfer mixture to a serving dish; chill for 2 hours. Makes 1 cup.

SAUCES

HOLLANDAISE SAUCE

4	**egg yolks**
1/2 teaspoon	**salt**
1/2 teaspoon	**dry mustard**
I tablespoon	**lemon juice**
pinch	**cayenne pepper**
1/4 pound	**butter,** melted

Place the egg yolks, salt, mustard, lemon juice, and cayenne in a
blender and blend for 3 seconds. Melt butter in a small saucepan.
Remove from heat and add blended mixture slowly, stirring constantly
with a whisk until thick. Serve with chicken or vegetables. Makes I cup.

APRICOT BARBECUE SAUCE

I can (16 ounces)	**apricots,** drained
1/4 cup	**firmly packed brown sugar**
I teaspoon	**cayenne pepper**
1/2 cup	**ketchup**
1/2 cup	**white vinegar**
2 teaspoons	**Worcestershire sauce**

Place all ingredients, in the order listed above, into a blender. Cover and blend on high until mixture is smooth. Makes 2 cups.

ROASTED RED PEPPER SAUCE

I jar (16 ounces)	**roasted red bell peppers**
$^1/_2$ teaspoon	**salt**
$^1/_4$ teaspoon	**garlic powder**
$^1/_8$ teaspoon	**ground red pepper**
I teaspoon	**olive oil**
I teaspoon	**paprika**
4 teaspoons	**lemon juice**

Place ingredients, in the order listed above, into a blender. Cover and blend on high until mixture is smooth. Makes 2 cups.

MARINARA SAUCE

2 tablespoons	**olive oil**
2 teaspoons	**minced garlic**
I teaspoon	**oregano**
I teaspoon	**basil**
I teaspoon	**garlic powder**
I tablespoon	**sugar**
dash	**salt**
dash	**pepper**
I can (6 ounces)	**tomato paste**
4	**tomatoes,** quartered
I	**medium onion,** quartered
I	**whole bay leaf**

Add all ingredients except bay leaf, in order listed above, into a blender. Blend for I minute, or until mixture is completely pureed. Pour into a large pot and add bay leaf. Bring mixture to a boil over medium heat. Boil for 5 minutes. Lower heat and simmer for 30 minutes, uncovered, stirring occasionally. Makes 2½ cups.

CRANBERRY SAUCE

1 cup	**fresh cranberries**
1	**apple,** cored and quartered
2/3 cup	**firmly packed dark brown sugar**
1/2 cup	**water**
1/4 cup	**chopped onion**
1 teaspoon	**ginger**
1 teaspoon	**curry powder**
1/8 teaspoon	**cayenne**

Place all ingredients, in order listed above, into a blender. Blend for 1 minute, or until mixture is completely pureed. Pour into a large pot and bring mixture to a boil over medium heat. Boil for 5 minutes. Lower heat and simmer for 30 minutes, uncovered, stirring occasionally. Makes 4–6 servings.

APPLESAUCE

4	**firm apples,** cored and quartered
1/4 cup	**water or orange juice**
1/4 cup	**sugar**
1/8 teaspoon	**cinnamon**

Place ingredients, in the order listed above, into a blender. Cover and blend on high until mixture is smooth. Transfer mixture to a serving dish and chill for 2 hours. Makes 2–4 servings.

CREAMY GREEN CHILE SAUCE

I	**onion,** quartered
I can (7 ounces)	**diced green chiles**
I tablespoon	**butter or margarine**
2 tablespoons	**flour**
$^3/_4$ cup	**chicken broth**
$^1/_2$ cup	**sour cream**
I tablespoon	**lime juice**
	salt, to taste

Sauté onion and chiles in butter until onions are clear. Place remaining ingredients in a blender, then add the onions. Cover and blend on high until mixture is smooth. Place in a saucepan and bring to a simmer. Serve over chicken or enchiladas. Makes I cup.

PESTO

2 cups	**fresh basil**
1/2 cup	**olive oil**
2 tablespoons	**pine nuts**
2 teaspoons	**minced garlic**
1 teaspoon	**salt**
1/2 cup	**grated Parmesan cheese**
2 tablespoons	**grated Romano cheese**
3 tablespoons	**butter**

Place all ingredients, in the order listed above, into a blender. Cover and blend on high until mixture is smooth. Serve with pasta, chicken, or as a spread on toasted bread. Makes 1 cup.

PEANUT SAUCE

¼ cup	**peanut butter**
¼ cup	**water**
3 tablespoons	**soy sauce**
2 tablespoons	**lime juice**
2 teaspoons	**minced garlic**
2 tablespoons	**rice vinegar**
2 teaspoons	**sugar**

Place peanut butter, water, and soy sauce in a microwavable bowl. Cover and heat on high for 2 minutes. Place all ingredients into a blender. Cover and blend on high until mixture is smooth. Serve with pasta or chicken. Makes 1 cup.

SWEET AND SOUR SAUCE

1/3 cup	**rice vinegar**
4 tablespoons	**brown sugar**
1 tablespoon	**ketchup**
1 teaspoon	**soy sauce**
1 can (8 ounces)	**pineapple chunks,** drained
2 teaspoons	**cornstarch**
4 teaspoons	**water**

Place vinegar, sugar, ketchup, soy sauce, and pineapple into a blender. Cover and blend on high until mixture is smooth. Mix together the cornstarch and water, add to the other ingredients; place over medium heat, stirring to thicken Makes 2 cups.

DESSERTS

MOIST CUPCAKES

¹/₂ cup	**unsalted butter,** softened
7 tablespoons	**sugar**
2 large	**eggs**
³/₄ cup	**self-rising cake flour**
¹/₂ teaspoon	**vanilla extract**
2–3 tablespoons	**milk**

Preheat oven to 400 degrees.

Place ingredients, in the order listed above, into a blender. Cover and blend until mixture is smooth, stopping and scraping sides as necessary. Line a muffin tin with baking cups and fill each with 2 heaping tablespoons batter. Bake for 15–20 minutes, or until golden. Makes 12 cupcakes.

CHOCOLATE CINNAMON CAKE

1 ½ cups	**sifted flour**
1 teaspoon	**baking powder**
½ teaspoon	**baking soda**
¼ teaspoon	**salt**
½ teaspoon	**cinnamon**
½ cup	**cocoa powder**
2	**eggs**
1 ¼ cups	**sugar**
½ cup	**shortening**
½ cup	**hot water**
1 ½ teaspoons	**vanilla**

Preheat oven to 350 degrees.

Grease an 8-inch square pan. Sift first 6 ingredients and set aside. Put remaining ingredients into a blender. Cover and blend until mixture is smooth, stopping and scraping sides as necessary. Add to flour mixture. Stir until just smooth. Pour batter into pan. Bake 35–40 minutes. Makes 6–8 servings.

CHOCOLATE DATE NUT CAKE

1 1/4 cups	**water**
1 cup	**chopped dates**
1 teaspoon	**baking soda**
2	**eggs**
3/4 cup	**oil**
1/2 teaspoon	**salt**
2 tablespoons	**cocoa**
1 cup	**sugar**
2 cups	**flour**
1/2 cup	**walnuts,** chopped
3 tablespoons	**sugar**
1 package (6 ounces)	**chocolate chips**

Preheat oven to 350 degrees.

In a microwavable bowl, place water, dates, and baking soda. Microwave on high for 2 minutes and then transfer to a blender. Add eggs, oil, salt, cocoa, and 1 cup sugar, then blend on high until creamy. Add flour and pulse until flour is mixed in. Pour into a greased 9 x 13-inch pan. Stir together walnuts, 3 tablespoons sugar, and chocolate chips and sprinkle over cake batter. Bake for 30–35 minutes. Makes 12–15 servings.

CHEESECAKE

8	**whole graham crackers**
1/4 cup	**sugar**
5 tablespoons	**butter or margarine,** melted
3 packages (8 ounces each)	**cream cheese,** softened
1 cup	**sugar**
3 large	**eggs**
1/2 cup	**sour cream**
2 tablespoons	**lemon juice**
1 1/2 tablespoons	**vanilla**

Preheat oven to 350 degrees.

Place graham crackers in a blender, 4 small rectangles at a time, until all are crumbled. Add sugar and butter and pulse until mixed. Press mixture into the bottom and up the sides of a 10-inch pie pan.

Blend cream cheese and sugar together until creamy; add eggs one at a time, blending well after each addition. Continue to blend while adding sour cream, lemon juice, and vanilla. Cover and blend until mixture is smooth, stopping and scraping sides as necessary. Pour filling over the crust and spread evenly. Bake for 1 hour and 15 minutes, or until top is set. Makes 8 servings.

BERRY MOUSSE

1 cup	**frozen, unsweetened whole strawberries,** thawed
1 package (8 ounces)	**cream cheese,** cubed
1/2 cup	**sifted powdered sugar**
1 cup	**whipped topping**

In a blender, combine the strawberries, cream cheese, and powdered sugar. Cover and blend until mixture is smooth, stopping and scraping sides as necessary. Pour into a mixing bowl and then fold in whipped topping. Spoon into dessert glasses and serve. Makes 6 servings.

CHOCOLATE MOUSSE

2 envelopes	**unflavored gelatin**
3/4 cup	**hot water**
I package (6 ounces)	**semisweet chocolate morsels**
I tablespoon	**sugar**
I cup	**heavy cream**
1/2 teaspoon	**vanilla**
I heaping cup	**crushed ice**

Combine gelatin and hot water in a blender at high speed for 40 seconds, scraping down sides once. Add chocolate and sugar. Cover and blend 10 seconds. Add cream, vanilla, and ice. Cover and blend at medium speed until ice dissolves and mixture begins to thicken. Pour immediately into dessert glasses. Chill until ready to serve. Makes 6 servings.

CRUSTLESS COCONUT PIE

2 cups	**milk**
4	**eggs**
2 cups	**sugar**
$^1/_2$ cup	**flour**
6 tablespoons	**butter or margarine,** softened
I teaspoon	**vanilla**
I cup	**coconut**

Preheat oven to 350 degrees.

Place all ingredients, in the order listed above, in a blender. Cover and blend until mixture is smooth, stopping and scraping sides as necessary. Pour into a greased and floured 10-inch pie plate. Bake for 50–60 minutes. Makes 8 servings.

BAKED CUSTARD

2 cups	**milk**
$^1/_2$ cup	**sugar**
4	**eggs**
2 teaspoons	**vanilla**
$^1/_4$ cup	**butter or margarine**
$^1/_2$ cup	**biscuit mix**

Preheat oven to 350 degrees.

Place all ingredients, in the order listed above, in a blender. Cover and blend until mixture is smooth, stopping and scraping sides as necessary. Pour into a greased 9-inch pie pan. Bake for 40 minutes. Makes 8 servings.

LEMON PIE

4	**eggs**
1/4 cup	**water**
6 tablespoons	**butter or margarine**
1	**lemon,** quartered, with peel
1 1/2 cups	**sugar**
1	**deep-dish pie shell,** prepared as directed

Preheat oven to 350 degrees.

Place all ingredients except the pie shell, in the order listed above, into a blender. Cover and blend on high until mixture is smooth. Pour into pie shell and bake for 45 minutes. Makes 8 servings.

PECAN PIE

2	**eggs**
²/₃ cup	**sugar**
¹/₂ teaspoon	**salt**
¹/₂ cup	**light corn syrup**
2 tablespoons	**butter or margarine,** melted
I teaspoon	**vanilla**
I cup	**pecans**
I (8-inch)	**unbaked pie shell**
I2	**pecan halves**

Preheat oven to 400 degrees.

Put eggs, sugar, salt, corn syrup, butter, and vanilla in a blender and blend well. Add I cup pecans and blend just enough to chop nuts coarsely. Pour into pie shell. Place pecan halves on top. Bake for about 30 minutes, or until golden brown. Makes 8 servings.

PUMPKIN PIE

I can (16 ounces)	**solid pack pumpkin**
I can (12 ounces)	**evaporated milk**
2	**eggs**
$^1/_2$ cup	**biscuit mix**
$^3/_4$ cup	**sugar**
$^1/_8$ teaspoon	**ground cloves**
$^1/_8$ teaspoon	**ground nutmeg**
I teaspoon	**cinnamon**
2 teaspoons	**vanilla**
I (9-inch)	**pie crust,** prepared as directed

Preheat oven to 350 degrees.

Place all ingredients except the pie crust, in the order listed above, into a blender. Cover and blend until mixture is smooth, stopping and scraping sides as necessary. Pour into pie crust and bake for 50–55 minutes, or until done. Makes 8 servings.

FRUITY ICE CREAM

I cup	**milk**
I teaspoon	**vanilla**
I teaspoon	**honey**
2 cups	**frozen fruit, such as berries, bananas, peaches, etc.**
	sugar, to taste

Place ingredients, in the order listed above, into a blender. Cover and blend on high until mixture is smooth. Divide into serving dishes and serve immediately or freeze to harden. Makes 2 servings.

STRAWBERRY ICE CREAM

1 tablespoon	**grated lemon peel**
1 tablespoon	**lemon juice**
1 package (10 ounces)	**frozen strawberries**
2/3 cup	**sweetened condensed milk**
1 cup	**whipped cream**

In a blender, combine all ingredients except whipped cream. Blend until creamy. Fold strawberry mixture into whipped cream, using rubber scraper or wire whisk. Serve immediately or freeze to harden. Makes 2–4 servings.

MINI NUT CAKES

2 cups	**flour,** sifted
2 1/2 teaspoons	**baking powder**
4	**eggs**
3/4 cup	**sugar**
1 cup	**hazelnuts or walnuts**
	shortening

Preheat oven to 350 degrees.

Sift together the flour and baking powder; set aside. Put eggs and sugar into a blender and mix until smooth. Add nuts and continue processing until nuts are finely ground. Add flour mixture all at once and pulse only until well mixed. Grease 12 muffin tins liberally with shortening. Scoop heaping spoonfuls of batter evenly into muffin tins. Bake for 20 minutes. Makes 12 servings.

FLAN

2 cups	**milk**
1/4 cup	**sugar**
1/8 teaspoon	**salt**
2	**eggs**
1/2 teaspoon	**vanilla**

Preheat oven to 325 degrees.

Place all ingredients, in the order listed above, into a blender and blend. Pour evenly into 6 small ramekins and place in a pan of hot water that goes halfway up the sides of the dishes. Bake for about 1 hour, or until a knife inserted into the center comes out clean. Remove from oven and chill until ready to serve. Makes 6 servings.

CHOCOLATE CHIP COOKIES

$1/2$ cup	**butter or margarine,** softened
$1/2$ cup	**peanut oil**
2	**eggs**
$1/2$ teaspoon	**salt**
1 teaspoon	**soda**
$1 1/2$ teaspoons	**vanilla**
1 cup	**white sugar**
$1/2$ cup	**brown sugar**
$2 1/4$ cups	**flour**
$1 1/2$ cups	**chocolate chips**

Preheat oven to 350 degrees.

Place first 8 ingredients into a blender and blend until smooth and creamy. Pour over flour and chocolate chips. Mix well and drop batter by heaping tablespoons onto a greased baking sheet. Bake for 10 minutes. Makes about 3 dozen cookies.

DRINKS

FROZEN LEMONADE

I	**lemon,** peeled, seeded, and cut into quarters
¹/₂ cup	**sugar**
2 cups	**water**
12	**ice cubes**

Place all ingredients, in the order listed above, into a blender. Cover and blend on high until mixture is smooth. Divide into glasses and serve immediately. Makes 2 servings.

STRAWBERRY MILK

1/2 cup	**strawberries**
2 cups	**milk**
2 teaspoons	**sugar**

Place all ingredients, in the order listed above, into a blender. Cover and blend on high until mixture is smooth. Pour into glasses and serve immediately. Makes 2 servings.

GRAPE FROTH

I can (6 ounces)	**grape juice concentrate**
I can	**water**
I pint	**lemon or lime sherbet**
I can (12 ounces)	**lemon-lime soda**

Place all ingredients, in the order listed above, into a blender. Cover and blend on high until mixture is smooth. Divide into glasses and serve immediately. Makes 4 servings.

ROOT BEER SMOOTHIE

I can (12 ounces)	**root beer**
I scoop	**vanilla ice cream**
2 cups	**ice**

Place all ingredients, in the order listed above, into a blender. Cover and blend on high until mixture is smooth. Serve immediately. Makes I serving.

PIÑA COLADA

	ice
1 cup	**coconut milk**
1 can (8 ounces)	**pineapple chunks**
2 tablespoons	**lemon juice**

Fill blender with ice. Place remaining ingredients, in the order listed above, into a blender. Cover and blend on high until mixture is smooth. Divide into glasses and serve immediately. Makes 4 servings.

ICED MOCHA

1 cup	**strong coffee,** cold
1 cup	**ice cubes**
1 cup	**chocolate ice cream**
$^1/_2$ cup	**milk**
$^1/_4$ teaspoon	**vanilla**

Place all ingredients, in the order listed above, into a blender. Cover and blend on high until mixture is smooth. Divide into glasses and serve immediately. Makes 2 servings.

PEAR-PINEAPPLE SMOOTHIE

1 can (12 ounces)	**pineapple juice**
1 can (8 ounces)	**pears,** with syrup
6	**ice cubes**

Place all ingredients, in the order listed above, into a blender. Cover and blend on high until mixture is smooth. Divide into glasses and serve immediately. Makes 4 servings.

FROZEN LEMON TEA

3 cups	**iced tea**
I can (6 ounces)	**lemonade concentrate**
I pint	**lemon sherbet**

Place all ingredients, in the order listed above, into a blender. Cover and blend on high until mixture is smooth. Divide into glasses and serve immediately. Makes 4 servings.

STRAWBERRY-
BANANA SMOOTHIE

1	**banana**
1/2 cup	**strawberries**
1 1/2 cups	**vanilla yogurt**
2 cups	**milk**

Place all ingredients, in the order listed above, into a blender. Cover and blend on high until mixture is smooth. Divide into glasses and serve immediately. Makes 2 servings.

CHOCOLATE MALT

2 1/4 cups	**milk**
3/4 cup	**chocolate syrup**
3 tablespoons	**malted milk powder**
4 cups	**vanilla ice cream**

Place all ingredients, in the order listed above, into a blender. Cover and blend on high until mixture is smooth. Divide into glasses and serve immediately. Makes 2 servings.

ORANGE JULIUS

12 ounces	**frozen orange juice concentrate**
2 cups	**milk**
2 cups	**water**
I cup	**sugar**
2 teaspoons	**vanilla extract**
	ice cubes, enough to fill blender

Place all ingredients, in the order listed above, into a blender. Cover and blend on high until mixture is smooth. Divide into glasses and serve immediately. Makes 4 servings.

CHOCOLATE SHAKE

2 cups **milk**
2 cups **vanilla ice cream**
3 tablespoons **chocolate syrup**

Place all ingredients, in the order listed above, into a blender. Cover and blend on high until mixture is smooth. Divide into glasses and serve immediately. Makes 2 servings.

STRAWBERRY COCOA-LICIOUS

1 cup	**ice**
1 cup	**strawberries**
1 cup	**apple juice**
1 teaspoon	**sugar**
1 teaspoon	**cocoa powder**

Place all ingredients, in the order listed above, into a blender. Cover and blend on high until mixture is smooth. Divide into glasses and serve immediately. Makes 2 servings.

HOT CHOCOLATE

³/₄ cup	**milk**
¹/₄ cup	**heavy cream**
¹/₄ cup	**marshmallows**
1 tablespoon	**chocolate sauce**

Heat milk and cream in microwave for 2 minutes. Pulse marshmallows in blender until chopped into small bits. Add chocolate sauce and hot milk and blend until mixed. Serve immediately. Makes 1 serving.

SPICY TOMATO BLEND

4 cups	**tomato juice**
1/2	**medium carrot**
1	**stalk celery**
1	**green onion**
1/2 cup	**Worcestershire sauce**
1	**lime,** quartered with peel on
2 tablespoons	**Tabasco sauce**
1 tablespoon	**cayenne**
1 tablespoon	**black pepper**
1 tablespoon	**celery salt**
2 tablespoons	**dill pickle juice**
1/4 cup	**fresh horseradish**

Place all ingredients, in the order listed above, into a blender. Cover and blend on high until mixture is smooth. Divide into glasses and serve immediately. Makes 4–5 servings.

ALL-NATURAL ENERGY DRINK

1	**medium carrot,** chopped
1	**apple,** cored and quartered
3	**oranges,** peeled
1	**banana,** peeled
12	**grapes**
6	**ice cubes**

Place all ingredients, in the order listed above, into a blender. Cover and blend on high until mixture is smooth. Pour into a glass and serve immediately. Makes 1 serving.

NOTES

METRIC CONVERSION CHART

Volume Measurements		Weight Measurements		Temperature Conversion	
U.S.	Metric	U.S.	Metric	Fahrenheit	Celsius
1 teaspoon	5 ml	1/2 ounce	15 g	250	120
1 tablespoon	15 ml	1 ounce	30 g	300	150
1/4 cup	60 ml	3 ounces	90 g	325	160
1/3 cup	75 ml	4 ounces	115 g	350	180
1/2 cup	125 ml	8 ounces	225 g	375	190
2/3 cup	150 ml	12 ounces	350 g	400	200
3/4 cup	175 ml	1 pound	450 g	425	220
1 cup	250 ml	2 1/4 pounds	1 kg	450	230

Yum! Check out these "101" favorites
for more tasty recipes:

Cake Mix	**Canned Soup**
More Cake Mix	**Slow Cooker**
Chocolate	**More Slow Cooker**
Gelatin	**BBQ**
Yogurt	**Casserole**
Pudding	**Dutch Oven**
Mac & Cheese	**Toaster Oven**
Ramen Noodles	**Chicken**
Salad	**Rotisserie Chicken**
Zucchini	**Ground Beef**
Tofu	**Meatballs**
Tortilla	**Grits**
Canned Biscuits	**Potato**

Each 128 pages, $9.99

Available at bookstores or directly
from GIBBS SMITH
1.800.835.4993
www.gibbs-smith.com

ABOUT THE AUTHOR

Toni Patrick, the culinary creative behind *101 Things to Do with Ramen Noodles, 101 Things to Do with Mac and Cheese* and *101 Things to Do with Canned Biscuits,* has masterfully blended quick cooking and good eating in her new book featuring the blender! Toni has been featured on the Food Network and was once named Irreverent Person of the Year by *Irreverent Magazine.* She lives in Walden, Colorado, with her daughter, Robbi.

$9.99 U.S.

101 Things To Do With a Blender

Make your next meal or treat in a snap—
just whirl, chop, or mix it in a blender!

Applesauce Muffins
French Onion Dip
Stuffed Zucchini
Cheeseburger Bake
Chocolate Cinnamon Cake
Pear-Pineapple Smoothie
And more!

COOKBOOK

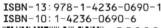

ISBN-13: 978-1-4236-0690-1
ISBN-10: 1-4236-0690-6

5 0 9 9 9

9 781423 606901

GIBBS SMITH
TO ENRICH AND INSPIRE HUMANKIND
WWW.GIBBS-SMITH.COM